D1550890

SPEARHEADS OF DEMOCRACY
Labor in the Developing Countries

Some Publications of the
COUNCIL ON FOREIGN RELATIONS

FOREIGN AFFAIRS (quarterly), edited by Hamilton Fish Armstrong.

THE UNITED STATES IN WORLD AFFAIRS (annually). Volumes for 1931, 1932 and 1933, by Walter Lippmann and William O. Scroggs; for 1934-1935, 1936, 1937, 1938, 1939 and 1940, by Whitney H. Shepardson and William O. Scroggs; for 1945-1947, 1947-1948 and 1948-1949, by John C. Campbell; for 1949, 1950, 1951, 1952, 1953 and 1954, by Richard P. Stebbins; for 1955, by Hollis W. Barber; for 1956, 1957, 1958, 1959, 1960 and 1961 by Richard P. Stebbins.

DOCUMENTS ON AMERICAN FOREIGN RELATIONS (annual). Volume for 1952 edited by Clarence W. Baier and Richard P. Stebbins; for 1953 and 1954, edited by Peter V. Curl; for 1955, 1956, 1957, 1958 and 1959, edited by Paul E. Zinner; for 1960 and 1961 edited by Richard P. Stebbins.

POLITICAL HANDBOOK OF THE WORLD (annual), edited by Walter H. Mallory.

THE LONG POLAR WATCH: Canada and the Defense of North America, by Melvin Conant.

LATIN AMERICA: Diplomacy and Reality, by Adolf A. Berle.

THE UNITED NATIONS: Structure for Peace, by Ernest A. Gross.

ARMS AND POLITICS IN LATIN AMERICA (Revised Edition) by Edwin Lieuwen.

THE FUTURE OF UNDERDEVELOPED COUNTRIES: Political Implications of Economic Development (Revised Edition) by Eugene Staley.

SPAIN AND DEFENSE OF THE WEST: Ally and Liability, by Arthur P. Whitaker.

SOCIAL CHANGE IN LATIN AMERICA TODAY: Its Implications for United States Policy, by Richard N. Adams, John P. Gillin, Allan R. Holmberg, Oscar Lewis, Richard W. Patch, and Charles W. Wagley.

FOREIGN POLICY: THE NEXT PHASE: The 1960s (Revised Edition), by Thomas K. Finletter.

DEFENSE OF THE MIDDLE EAST: Problems of American Policy (Revised Edition), by John C. Campbell.

COMMUNIST CHINA AND ASIA: Challenge to American Policy, by A. Doak Barnett.

FRANCE, TROUBLED ALLY: De Gaulle's Heritage and Prospects, by Edgar S. Furniss, Jr.

THE SCHUMAN PLAN: A Study in Economic Cooperation, 1950-1959, by William Diebold, Jr.

SOVIET ECONOMIC AID: The New Aid and Trade Policy in Underdeveloped Countries, by Joseph S. Berliner.

RAW MATERIALS: A Study of American Policy, by Percy W. Bidwell.

NATO AND THE FUTURE OF EUROPE, by Ben T. Moore.

INDIA AND AMERICA: A Study of Their Relations, by Phillips Talbot and S. L. Poplai.

JAPAN BETWEEN EAST AND WEST, by Hugh Borton, Jerome B. Cohen, William J. Jorden, Donald Keene, Paul F. Langer and C. Martin Wilbur.

NUCLEAR WEAPONS AND FOREIGN POLICY, by Henry A. Kissinger.

MOSCOW-PEKING AXIS: Strengths and Strains, by Howard L. Boorman, Alexander Eckstein; Philip E. Mosely and Benjamin Schwartz.

CLIMATE AND ECONOMIC DEVELOPMENT IN THE TROPICS, by Douglas H. K. Lee.

WHAT THE TARIFF MEANS TO AMERICAN INDUSTRIES, by Percy W. Bidwell.

RUSSIA AND AMERICA: Dangers and Prospects, by Henry L. Roberts.

FOREIGN AFFAIRS BIBLIOGRAPHY, 1942-1952, by Henry L. Roberts.

SPEARHEADS OF
DEMOCRACY
Labor in the Developing Countries

by

G E O R G E   C.   L O D G E

Published for the
Council on Foreign Relations
by
Harper & Row, Publishers · *New York and Evanston*

The Council on Foreign Relations is a non-profit institution devoted to study of the international aspects of American political, economic and strategic problems. It takes no stand, expressed or implied, on American policy.

The authors of books published under the auspices of the Council are responsible for their statements of fact and expressions of opinion. The Council is responsible only for determining that they should be presented to the public.

SPEARHEADS OF DEMOCRACY: LABOR IN THE DEVELOPING
COUNTRIES

*Copyright, © 1962, by Council on Foreign Relations, Inc.
All rights reserved, including the right to reproduce
this book or any portion thereof in any form.
For information, address Council on Foreign Relations,
58 East 68th Street, New York 21*

FIRST EDITION

*Library of Congress catalog card number: 62-17129
Printed in the United States of America
by Quinn & Boden Company, Inc., Rahway, N. J.
Published by Harper & Row, Publishers, Incorporated*

ACKNOWLEDGMENTS

First and foremost, I am deeply grateful to the Council on Foreign Relations which has made the publication of this book possible and helped so much with its production. I owe a special debt to the members of the Council's study group who gave careful consideration to the manuscript and made many helpful suggestions. Probably none of them agrees fully with all my arguments, and they have no responsibility for the views set out in this book. Paul M. Herzog, the group's chairman, deserves my particular thanks for the effective way he presided over some spirited discussions. The group included Robert J. Alexander, Solomon Barkin, John C. Campbell, Gordon Chapman, William Diebold, Jr., John Fayerweather, George S. Franklin, Jr., Howard C. Johnson, the late Jay B. Krane, Isador Lubin, Porter McKeever, Cord Meyer, Jr., Ben T. Moore, Vernon O'Rourke, Walter J. Sedwitz, Arnold L. Steinbach, George L-P Weaver, and John P. Windmuller.

Special thanks are due William Diebold, Jr., Senior Research Fellow at the Council, with whom I first discussed this book; and to my successor, Assistant Secretary of Labor George L-P Weaver, whose cooperation, assistance, and long experience in international matters have been of exceptional value to me. I know that many of the criticisms and recommendations which I have made in this book are of equal concern to Mr. Weaver, and that he, undoubtedly more effectively than I, is working to solve the problem raised.

This book could not have been written without the assistance of my associates in the Department of Labor. At the risk of omitting many who made a very real contribution, I should like to mention several who read the entire text and offered exceptionally valuable comments and criticisms: Joaquin Bazan, Howard Carpenter, John Condon, Leonard Linsenmayer, James Hoover, Joseph Judge, Daniel Lazorchick, William Gerber, Arnold Steinbach, Lester Trachtman, Morris Weisz, and Frances Hicks. At a late stage, Mr. Steinbach and William McIntire helped by checking certain facts and quotations.

I am also extremely grateful to my friends in the American labor movement who assisted greatly by reading the manuscript, especially Michael Ross, Director of the International Affairs Department of the American Federation of Labor—Congress of Industrial Organizations, Serafino Romualdi, Inter-American Representative of the AFL-CIO, and Harry Pollak, member, International Department of the AFL-CIO.

My thanks also to Richard Davies, Executive Director of Klein & Saks, management consultants, for reading and commenting on Chapter V regarding American management's foreign operations; to Clarence Randall for his highly perceptive comments on Chapter I; and to Brian Fane, British labor attaché.

Joseph E. Johnson, President of the Carnegie Endowment for International Peace, read the manuscript and made a number of useful sugggestions.

I am indebted as well to the Dean and Faculty of the Harvard School of Business Administration for allowing me to complete the manuscript while lecturing at the School. There could not have been a more stimulating or sympathetic environment in which to work. I am particularly grateful to my secretary, Mrs. Harold Siegel, for her tireless and capable efforts. Antoinette Rogers of the staff of the Council on Foreign Relations prepared the manuscript for the press and made the index. Lorna Brennan and her staff at the Council helped greatly in putting the book through several drafts.

While I am grateful for the assistance I have received from these friends and associates, responsibility for the contents of this book is mine.

I should like to thank my father, Henry Cabot Lodge, who read the entire manuscript, giving me the benefit of his many years of experience in foreign affairs.

My wife, Nancy Kunhardt Lodge, has my deepest gratitude for her patience and understanding during the difficulties and irritations of composition. Her assistance and devotion were as essential to this book as they are to the author's life.

G. C. L.

June 1962

CONTENTS

INTRODUCTION

Shortly after he took office, Secretary of State Dean Rusk spoke to his colleagues in the State Department as follows:

Older political forms have disintegrated. New international forms are coming into being. We are experiencing enormous pressures to achieve economic and social improvements in all parts of the world, as masses of people who have largely been isolated from currents of world opinion, knowledge, and information are coming to realize that their miseries are not a part of an ordained environment about which nothing can be done. . . .

What we in the United States do or do not do will make a very large difference in what happens in the rest of the world. We . . . must think about foreign policy in its total context. We cannot regard foreign policy as something left over after defense policy or trade policy or fiscal policy [and, I would add, labor policy—G. C. L.] has been extracted. Foreign policy is the total involvement of the American people with peoples and governments abroad.[1]

We are involved in a total war. It cannot be won easily or cheaply. In fact, it cannot be won without the total mobilization of all our resources and the sharp focus of those resources upon the priorities which the national interest

[1] Informal remarks to State Department policy-making officers, reprinted in *The Department of State Bulletin*, March 20, 1961, pp. 395, 396.

may set. This means a total commitment by all Americans. I believe we are prepared to make this commitment if we know how.

This book is a plea to government, management, and labor to perceive more precisely than they have the importance of organizations of workers in the developing world to the fulfillment of U.S. foreign policy and the objectives of the free world. To paraphrase Mr. Rusk, foreign policy is not "something left over" after the consideration of labor's role in Asia, Africa, and Latin America has been taken out. In fact, our foreign policy cannot be successful unless it specifically includes and gives high priority to the activities of worker organizations in these vast areas.

Our government currently is woefully ill-equipped to deal with international labor affairs. The various departments and agencies involved have gone their own way with little regard for the whole effect and there has been a deplorable lack of imaginative thought at high levels. Government has fretted and fumed as crises appear over the desk's edge. It has built little bureaucratic nests, cradling jealousy, useless jobs, and foot-dragging. It has from time to time piously stated the obvious. But little has been done to make those engaged in the vast array of U.S. foreign operations aware of the problem, or to arrange governmental resources so as to take advantage of the opportunities offered.

American management feels little pressure from Washington to behave itself abroad, and what pressure there is can generally be disregarded with impunity. While generally our foreign enterprise has promoted the best interests of the United States, providing useful capital, skills, and business methods to aid the economic growth of less-developed countries, in too many cases it has left its best practices at the water's edge and sacrificed the national interest in favor of the stockholders', failing to realize that both are one. Too often American companies have failed to understand clearly the role of a worker organization in a developing country, its purposes and requirements and its usefulness to society and the company. Regarding it as an adversary to be overcome or at least weakened to submissiveness, the company sometimes produces good evidence to support the theory of class struggle. In so doing it misses the opportunity to build a relationship and an institution which in time of instability and trouble might save its neck.

American labor, divided within itself and at odds with its principal allies abroad, has failed to do all it might to provide effective leadership in the fight against Communist subversion in Asia, Africa, and Latin America. While we must be grateful for its great contribution, there is much more that can be done, given more adequate staff and better coordinated direction of international activities.

All three—American government, business, and labor— need a heightened sense of the totality of the struggle in which we are engaged. But this sense will lead to nothing but frustration if there is not the over-all leadership to fix the objectives and lay down the means to their fulfillment.

Note: The following abbreviations are frequently used.

AATUF, All-African Trade Union Federation
ACFTU, All-China Federation of Trade Unions
AFL, American Federation of Labor
AFRO, African Regional Organization
AID, Agency for International Development
AITUC, All-India Trade Union Congress
ATUC, African Trade Union Confederation
CATU, Confederation of Arab Trade Unions
CIO, Congress of Industrial Organizations
CTAL, Confederation of Latin American Workers
HMS, Hind Mazdoor Sabha
ICATU, International Confederation of Arab Trade Unions
ICFTU, International Confederation of Free Trade Unions
IFCTU, International Federation of Christian Trade Unions
IFPAAW, International Federation of Plantation, Agricultural, and
    Allied Workers
ILO, International Labor Organization
INTUC, Indian National Trade Union Congress
ITS, International Trade Secretariat(s)
IWW, International Workers of the World
KANU, Kenya African National Union
KBKI, Indonesian labor federation
ORIT, Inter-American Regional Organization of Workers
PBKA, Indonesian railway workers
SOBSI, All-Indonesian Central Labor Organization
SOHYO, Japanese labor federation
UGTAN, Union Générale des Travailleurs d'Afrique Noire
UGTT, Union Générale Tunisienne du Travail
WFTU, World Federation of Trade Unions

SPEARHEADS OF DEMOCRACY

Labor in the Developing Countries

Chapter I

REVOLT AND REFORM

The world today is shaken by far-reaching revolutionary changes which demand continual and sensitive examination of our national objectives and of the means to accomplish them. No preoccupation with the East-West "stalemate" should delude us into supposing that the world at large is in any sense stalemated. Quite the reverse, it is moving with breath-taking speed in a variety of directions, disrupting economic, political, social, and ideological patterns which for thousands of years have provided some measure of stability.

A look ahead reveals the stark possibility that man, having achieved the ability to destroy himself entirely, may proceed to do so. We also can dimly see, however, the edges of a glorious vision, the possibility of an entirely new environment wherein we may harness our fantastic skill for the betterment of all men, alleviate the hunger and agony of two-thirds of the human race, help in the establishment of stable and just political systems throughout the world based on the will of the people, and play a part in man's continuing evolution into a more nearly perfect creature through increasing spiritual consciousness.

The unsettling circumstances continually arising around

the world, whether in the Congo, Cuba, Laos, or Viet-Nam, should not cause us despair; nor can we afford to dismiss them as unimportant outbursts safely removed from our shores; nor should we blame them all on Khrushchev. They are the perfectly logical results of violent movements for change which are pervading the lives of virtually all of the world's people and shaking the foundations of the past. To promote our foreign policy, to protect the independence of nations and improve the lot of mankind, we must make quite sure we understand these movements clearly and perceive the powerful forces moving in and through them.

They arise from several sources. First, there is the determined desire on the part of virtually all the nations of Latin America, Asia, and Africa to increase rapidly their industrial and agricultural production so that individual incomes may rise above the pitifully low levels of today—less than $100 a year in many countries—and so that their people can have food to eat, a house in which to live, education for their children, and other necessities for the good life.

This is both necessary and inevitable. In the developing portions of the world, where two-thirds of the human race lives, four out of five families are still forced to scratch their subsistence from the earth. Life expectancy is between thirty and forty years. Nutrition is low, the conditions of health are bad. Such an imbalance between rich and poor causes deep resentment, and helps to fire the second great force sweeping the newly developing world: the insistence on national independence and self-determination in all matters. It should be clearly understood that political independence is not enough; freedom from colonial bondage is not enough; there is deep down a yearning for economic independence. There is the persistent gripe, however unjustified, that for hundreds of years the industrialized nations of Europe and North America have plundered the poor nations of Asia, Africa, and Latin America, exploited their peoples, pillaged their natural resources, taken what they could and left little but poverty and ignorance behind.

International communism offers to show the way to the fulfillment of these deep desires. We must recognize that the Communist appeal, particularly in the newly developing countries, is in large part an emotional one and cannot be argued logically. The masses of people, and more especially their leaders, are impressed by what the Soviet Union has done for itself in forty years. To many of these people, communism represents a new mystical, indescribable hope which appeals to their hearts. To be sure, there is some concern about replacing one form of colonialism with another and more terrible variety. The imperialist character of the Soviet Union is becoming more and more evident to some leaders. But to people in urgent need of the minimal requirements to sustain life, the danger signals are frequently obscured.

Against this background the United States comes forward with its stirring and revolutionary message that all men are created equal and endowed with rights to life, liberty, and the pursuit of happiness. This is without doubt the most powerful ideology abroad in the world today, but it requires our loyalty and devotion. The fulfillment of our foreign policy requires that we support effectively and enthusiastically the legitimate demands of the peoples of the newly developing world for social justice, for economic self-reliance, for freedom from dictatorship of whatever sort: Communist, military, plutocratic, or any other variety. This is not always easy. For military or diplomatic reasons we have frequently found ourselves supporting individuals, elites, and oligarchies who are completely unsympathetic to our purposes as set forth in the Declaration of Independence. We cannot wonder that such inconsistency confuses. Sustaining the status quo merely because it is the status quo, when it is not in harmony with the just interests of the people, may be orthodox nineteenth-century diplomatic practice but it is not a valid theory of operations in this age of revolution.

So it is that American foreign policy has become a much more complicated business than it was fifty years ago when diplomatic relations were largely between the embassy and the palace. Our foreign affairs involve infinitely more than the protection of American citizens and their property abroad by a select group of diplomats.[1] Now our survival as a nation is closely linked with the cause of freedom in the world and the dignity of men everywhere as objectives of United States foreign policy. We have a total commitment involving the lives of us all. More than one and a half million Americans are now living and working abroad, for the government, private companies, foundations, labor unions, and churches.[2] Each is a factor in the image of our country. Each promotes or detracts from the fulfillment of our purposes.

There once was a time when the principal support for diplomacy was military might, the "big stick." While our armed force is still of the utmost importance as a retaliatory threat for defense against aggression, it does not provide the means of accomplishing all our objectives abroad. While we are indeed engaged in a war for the achievement of our objectives, some of the battlefields are strange ones: the rice fields of Indonesia, the factories and villages of India, the mines of Africa, the oil wells of Venezuela, and the plantations of Costa Rica. And the enemy appears in unusual shapes and forms: the child dying of malaria in a hut by the Nile, the grandfather begging for life on the streets of Calcutta, the dictator, the firing squad, the exploiter.

So it is that we are turning increasingly to economic and

[1] Employees of the Department of State in 1900 numbered 865 and in 1939 only 2,738, compared to 13,632 in 1961. This figure does not include USIA or ICA (now AID) employees.

[2] Harlan Cleveland, Gerard J. Mangone, and John Clarke Adams, *The Overseas Americans* (New York: McGraw-Hill, 1960), p. 3.

social tools for the implementation of our foreign policy. So it is that the whole panoply of economic aid and technical assistance programs have been developed. These, in the spirit of what Edgar Faure called "selfish altruism," are designed to promote our interests and those of freedom, having in mind the vital forces at work in the world today. In his foreign aid message to Congress on March 22, 1961, President Kennedy said, quite rightly: "The economic collapse of those free but less-developed nations which now stand poised between sustained growth and economic chaos would be disastrous to our national security, harmful to our comparative prosperity, and offensive to our conscience." But he said further: "Existing foreign aid programs and concepts are largely unsatisfactory and unsuited for our needs and for the needs of the underdeveloped world as it enters the sixties."

There are a number of reasons why our efforts to commit our resources to promoting economic development abroad have been, to use the President's word, "unsatisfactory." Perhaps most important is that we have not fully understood that, in the countries we are aiding, economic growth, a higher gross national product, an increased capital investment, do not necessarily mean progress or the fulfillment of U.S. objectives. An increase in the wealth of a nation can cause a variety of extremely nonprogressive results. The rich may get richer and the poor, poorer. There may be more Cadillacs and bathtubs for the few, or more cosmetics and face tissues for the many. The new wealth may accumulate in the hands of a few politicians, or it may be frittered away uselessly. We are now realizing that our objectives of peace, self-determination, and an improved standard of living for all depend principally on the existence of social, political, and economic organizations, institutions, and machinery necessary to ensure sound development with social justice and maximum freedom. Such a structure is necessary before economic aid can flow in useful channels and produce the results we intend. Its erection demands social and economic reform in many countries and, if aid is given without such reform, it may well do more harm than good by perpetuating an exploitative and repressive system. Aid given without reform can, in fact, directly benefit our enemies.

The United States for some time, unfortunately, tended to think of aid to the developing world in much the same terms as it thought of aid given under the Marshall Plan to devastated Europe following World War II. Despite the devastation, Europe in 1948 had a highly sophisticated and well-developed social and economic structure which was just waiting to be fattened with funds and material. It had large supplies of skilled manpower, long experience with democratic procedures, and great potential resources. In contrast, in most of the less-developed world eight out of ten people cannot read or write. There is virtually no middle class. Social and economic organizations are primitive and in many cases society is ruled by an oligarchy: the army, wealthy landowners, or a handful of politicians. In such a society economic growth brings progress only if that growth takes place in a political and social structure that expresses the best interests of the whole country.

The Communists, of course, can produce excellent examples of economic development. Certainly a Soviet dam holds back as much water as one of ours. Their tractors are without doubt as useful. But the growth they bring is unacceptable to free societies if it is accompanied by bondage.

The principal reason why our economic aid programs have been unsatisfactory, then, is that we have paid insufficient attention to the permanent institutions and organizations which must form a prelude to successful development. Similarly, the principal reason why some of the foreign operations of American business are subject to criticism and are harmful to our national interest is that too often our businessman in a developing country fails to understand or deliberately ignores the basic needs and problems of the country. Too often he is more interested in a quick and profitable return on investment than in contributing to the formation of a strong, healthy, social and economic structure. Too often he fails to see that his own interests as well as those of the United States are jeopardized by such shortsightedness.

This is the setting within which our foreign policy objectives must be achieved. This is the environment of our foreign operations. This is the world and these are the challenges which we face today.

It is a world in revolution. This is no revolution of the elite. It is a revolution broadly based and deeply felt among the masses of the underdeveloped countries who make up most of the world's population. Although frequently led by intellectuals, it is a revolution forced by working people, including, of course, peasants and farmers.

Thus it is that among the most important elements in the political, economic, and social structure of the newly developing countries of Asia, Africa, and Latin America are the organizations which these workers have formed to help them pursue their objectives more vigorously and effectively. Thus it is that workers' organizations or trade unions have come to be of central and critical importance in the world struggle today. They are frequently the spearhead in the drive for freedom, independence, social justice, reform, education, and political liberty throughout the developing world.

The obscure trade unionist of today may well be the president or prime minister of tomorrow. In many countries of Asia, Africa, and Latin America trade unions are almost the only organized force in direct contact with the people and they are frequently among the most important influences on the people. They are often the most effective means for the expression of the people's determined desire for material improvement and political justice. They are primary targets for Communist subversion and control. And they are, at the same time, the first line of defense against communism and other forms of totalitarianism. In fact they have shown themselves in many countries to be the most alert and effective indigenous organizations in resisting Moscow's colonialism.

While in many parts of the world the economic importance of worker organizations may be slight, invariably their political potential is substantial. We in the United States, of course, are in no position to control their activities, but whether we like it or not, many of our private and governmental actions do, in fact, affect these organizations and vice versa. In any case, we must be keenly aware of them as we are of other sources of power, such as the military, a political party, or an oligarchical clique. Although worker organizations in some places are forces for progress, they are also sometimes tools of the state, used to implement domestic control or foreign policy. Whatever may be their role, their activities are usually important to the fulfillment of United States foreign policy.

This book is about these organizations, what they do, how they do it, who their leaders are, what their significance is to the United States, and what our policy should be toward them. This is a new subject. It is one to which the government has given little attention. It is a difficult matter for the government, in fact, because most U.S. dealings with these organizations are through our own labor movement or American private companies operating overseas. But these dealings are quite obviously of the utmost importance to the government and to our national interest generally.

Only recently have we begun to see the importance of these organizations and the difficulties and opportunities which they present to us. But now all of a sudden a number of questions are arising which need thoughtful answers.

To what extent, for instance, should our government's decision on whether or not to assist India in the construction of a fourth national steel plant be affected by the vital struggle between Communist and non-Communist trade unions in industrial India? Would such an effort on our part tend to strengthen the non-Communist unions? If so, how best could that end be accomplished?

Assuming it is our international policy, as it is our national policy—set out in the preamble of the Taft-Hartley Act—to encourage the growth of strong, free, democratic trade unions, is it realistic to suppose that unions in a rapidly industrializing less-developed country can follow the same patterns of development as did the trade unions of Europe and the United States? Or is there a different route to their effective development? Do the pressures of economic development impose special burdens on all elements of the society, including trade unions?

What is the relationship between political parties and trade unions in the developing world? What implications does this have for U.S. policy and programs?

What is the "image of America" to labor abroad? How can it be improved? What, for example, might be done to correct some of the misapprehensions now held by the anti-American but extremely powerful Socialist trade unions of Japan? Do visits to this country help?

What of the American company whose industrial relations practices abroad are a serious deterrent to the achievement of U.S. policy?

Is the government presently organized to deal properly with questions of international labor affairs? And the same

question could be asked about the American labor movement.

These are a few of the problems which will be explored
in the following chapters, wherein I will seek to consider
concretely some of the strengths and weaknesses of our
position and to suggest new lines of approach.

Chapter II

LABOR'S ROLE IN NEWLY DEVELOPING COUNTRIES

The activities and functions of workers' organizations in newly developing countries are many and varied. To attempt to generalize about them is dangerous. Their characteristics are molded by the level of economic development of each particular country, by the attitude of the government, by the caliber and nature of their leadership, by the intensity of Communist pressure upon them, and by many other factors. But there are some generalizations which are useful in considering the relationship of these organizations to the fulfillment of United States foreign policy.

In the first place workers' organizations in some form are basic, inevitable, and permanent. They may be suppressed or taken over by an authoritarian regime, but they are rarely totally extinguished. And many times they rise, invigorated by suppression.

The workers' organizations of the developing world are sustained by the determined desire of the people for an improvement in their way of life, for a square meal where there has been starvation, for a hospital bed where there have been disease and death, for a decent house where there have been filth and squalor, for freedom and dignity where there have been domination and servility. Their roots lie deep in the hearts of the people, and, while their membership may be small, they are the first true, wholly indigenous and national organizations which many of the peoples of Asia and Africa, as well as some in Latin America, have ever known.

The Communists realize their significance full well. They are making great efforts to win over not only government or business officials, who may be here today and gone tomorrow, but union leaders, who, by the very nature of their organizations, are likely to grow in influence as industrialization progresses. We would be seriously deluding ourselves if we did not realize that while the Communists have had their ups and downs, they have increased substantially their influence in many labor movements of Asia, Africa, and Latin America. They are concentrating on getting control of the workers in key industries throughout the newly developing nations. Large numbers of young leaders are invited to Moscow each year for a highly developed course of indoctrination. When these men return to their native land, they are revered if for no other reason than that they have been far off in an airplane, an experience which few have had. They are frequently admired and listened to when they preach that the way to quick development, easy money, and full bellies is not through the slow uneven processes of democracy or the complicated and misunderstood devices of "free enterprise," but by the shorter Russian route of totalitarianism, which has accomplished wonders in a few decades.

It is misleading to think of the workers' organizations of the underdeveloped countries as bearing any close resemblance to labor unions in the United States today. For the most part, they exist in the midst of poverty, illiteracy, and instability. Generally, labor organizations in the newly developing world were superimposed on a not unreceptive rural society for political or ideological reasons—independence, freedom from discrimination, and as primitive agents for the achievement of individual dignity. They have developed as mutual aid societies, rural cooperatives, social welfare organizations, semifraternal groups, and perhaps most important, as adjuncts to political parties. Sometimes, as in India and Algeria, they were deliberately created as part of a nationalist movement. In a few instances, industrial unions comparable to our own have emerged, particularly in Latin America, in the mining, oil, and textile industries. Increasingly, labor unions in a number of countries are attempting to ease the transition for young workers coming off the farms and out of the bush to work in the cities and towns. This transition, representing as it frequently does, a staggering change, often telescoping thousands of years, is one of the most unsettling influences at work today in Asia, Africa, and Latin America. Worker organizations have a great opportunity to offer at least some aid and comfort to the expectant youths of these areas who come to the big city in search of fortune and too often find unemployment, misery, and frustration.

Unions in the developing countries were not the result of worker initiative and could not have been, given the economic and political environment in which they emerged. They did not spring from mass initiative. Rather they were held out to a hitherto unorganized populace by political parties, governments, reformers, and intellectuals of all sorts. Many union movements were started in colonial territories by Europeans, sometimes as elements of local control, sometimes by labor organizers from the mother countries. It was the British who founded the labor movements in Ghana, Nigeria, East Africa, India, and Singapore; the French those in Guinea, French West Africa, and Viet-Nam, for example. But at the same time these organizations have gained their real strength as agents of nationalism, becoming the spearhead of anticolonial movements, striking out violently at all who obstruct independence. Their growth has also been influenced by humanitarian and ideological forces, including socialism, Marxism, and communism. Some were formed for prestige purposes in the belief that a trade union is a status symbol which must adorn any modern society.

The Different History of American Labor

Workers' organizations in the underdeveloped countries bear little resemblance to American trade unions today, largely because of the great differences between the social, economic, and political development of our country and that of the newly emerging world. We must remember, for example, that our country has never known feudalism. Land for us has generally been plentiful, good, and cheap. It has not been controlled by a handful of powerful individuals. We have had a government which responded, however imperfectly, to the public consensus. This has made it unnecessary and in fact inadvisable for American labor, during most of its history, to seek to achieve its objectives by forming a political party or advocating a basic change in the system. We have been blessed by ready supplies of rich natural resources. Because of immigration from industrial Europe and our early attention to public education we have always had an unusually high level of literacy and technical skill. Perhaps most important, our people have, by and large, always had enough to eat. A full stomach, I am sure, has a lot to do with what we regard as our traditional virtues of initiative, self-reliance, and energy. These are all characteristics that are hard to find in today's developing countries where forms of feudalism, oligarchy, dictatorship, ignorance, poverty, and starvation have been the rule rather than the exception. It is no wonder that in seeking to improve the welfare of workers in the face of these evils, labor unions abroad have developed into quite different social engines.

But we ignore a significant fact of history when we fail to recognize that in our early stages of development as a nation, worker organizations played a significant role and one surprisingly similar to that of labor unions in newly developing countries today. One of our weaknesses in presenting an understandable and persuasive image of America to the emerging countries has been our failure to see ourselves as we were in 1776 and the years immediately thereafter. Our revolution with its Declaration of Independence is still the most important ideological event in modern times. If we deny it or blur it or fail to make its meaning explicit today, we are denying ourselves our most valuable asset. I was never more aware of this than at a meeting of the International Labor Organization in Geneva where a young African trade-union leader from a country which had just won its independence came to me, his eyes blazing with intensity, to ask detailed questions about our revolution and its aftermath. Sorely worried about Communist inroads in his country, he said that what he wanted more than anything to save his country's freedom were copies of *The Federalist* papers. These to him were more valuable at that moment than any amount of money, technical assistance, or vague talk.

We should not forget that the workers in colonial America played an important role in our fight for political liberty.[1] As in the newly developing world today, the worker organizations of early America were formed for mutual aid, political agitation, and over-all improvement. They included both

[1] Foster Rhea Dulles, *Labor in America* (New York: Crowell, 1955), pp. 15, 16.

journeymen and masters. They provided sickness and death benefits and filled other social needs in a rudimentary fashion. They were made up largely of artisans, mechanics, and tradesmen, who together formed a relatively important intellectual group within the community, as they do today in many newly developing countries. They were men who were oppressed not only by the British but by native upper classes. They organized to assert all their rights—political as well as economic and social.

"The role of small tradesmen, artisans and mechanics in promoting the revolutionary cause was particularly important in Massachusetts," writes Foster Rhea Dulles in *Labor in America*. "Again and again when the ardor of merchants and farmers appeared to be subsiding, the 'rage of patriotism' was stimulated by the zeal of those whom the Tories derisively called the 'Mobility' or the 'Rabble.' The popular party in Boston, so astutely led by Samuel Adams, was in large part made up of wharfingers, shipwrights, bricklayers, weavers and tanners who were equally opposed to rule by British officials or colonial aristocrats. The Sons of Liberty, and later the local Committees of Correspondence, were generally recruited from workers from the docks, shipyards and ropewalks. The famous 'Loyall Nine,' which was to instigate the mob action that led to the Boston Massacre and the Boston Tea Party, included two distillers, two braziers, a printer, a jeweler, a painter and a ship captain."

Our early worker organizations were in the forefront of our heroic fight for independence. The Ancient and Honorable Mechanical Company of Baltimore, the Firemen's Association of Charleston, the Heart-and-Hand Fire Company of Philadelphia were the revolutionary centers in those cities. Their zeal often aroused conservative fears that the revolutionary movement was going too far. "The heads of the mobility [*sic*] grow dangerous to the gentry," wrote

Gouverneur Morris, "and how to keep them down is the question."[2]

In the 1820s American unions grew substantially in strength and influence. After the depression of 1819 working conditions got progressively worse. Workers began to doubt the promise of the revolution. There were strikes and violence. When a carpenters' strike to get a ten-hour day failed, unions resorted to political action. Here again the similarity to events today in newly developing countries is worth noting. A widespread political movement of workingmen's parties grew up. Workers began to lose faith in the government, feeling it was on the side of the aristocracy.[3] Armed with the vote, they formed their own parties and played an important part in electing Jackson in 1828 and in making "the Jacksonian revolution." The New York Workingmen's party had a deep effect on American politics, fighting as it did for public education, the abolition of debtors' prison, and legislative reforms for shorter hours and higher wages.

Early American labor history is filled with examples of close alliance between unions and political parties, of agitation for reform by government, by political means and not merely economic, even for the overthrow of the existing order. The National Labor Union in 1866 had as its slogan: "Let our cry be reform. Down with the monied aristocracy." This tradition continued into the Socialist movements of the nineteenth and twentieth centuries, the "Black International," and the IWW.

Samuel Gompers and the founders of the American Federation of Labor saw, however, that direct political action on behalf of one party or another was not to be the way that American organized labor could have maximum effect. By 1890, when the American Federation of Labor was

[2] Quoted in same, p. 16.
[3] Same, p. 36.

formed, many of the political reforms in which labor was particularly interested had already taken place, and, more importantly, it had been amply demonstrated that an alliance between a trade union and a political party in the United States weakened both. Although he was nurtured in European socialism, Gompers was keenly aware of the unique and revolutionary character of American society. He was unalterably opposed to socialism and to radical change of the existing economic and political system. So it was that American labor came to be first of all a basically conservative force in American politics, relying for its gains on independent economic action against employers through collective bargaining rather than political action by the state.

This decision was a long time in the making. The issue was not even clearly settled by World War I, when Socialist trade-union leaders were active and inspired a large following, especially among textile workers. So in judging the worker organizations of newly developing countries it behooves us to be mindful of our whole history and not only that part which is most recent.

International communism has over a long period of years sought to use organizations of workers as instruments for the seizure of political power. In a significant number of new nations, however, as in the United States, the strongest anti-Communist elements have come to be the labor unions. As in our country during the 1930s and after World War II, around the world trade unions have been among the first organized forces to realize that with communism comes not utopia but a new and more dreadful form of exploitation. We should never forget that the Hungarian revolt in 1956 was organized and led by the workers' councils in the factories of Budapest.

In India the free trade unions are fighting a desperate battle against the Communist-controlled All-India Trade Union Congress for control of the work force in strategic areas, including the steel industry, and on the railroads, docks, and plantations. It is important to note here that when we speak of trade unions in less-developed countries, we are not only referring to unions in services, manufacturing, and mining. In fact, plantation workers are among the most important organizations in the newly developing world. The members of the powerful Malayan plantation workers' union, for example, were a key force in preserving the independence of their country in 1948. Coming largely from the jungles and mountains, they were exposed firsthand to the ruthless methods of Communist imperialism. They saw their huts burned, their wives and children nailed to trees, and their country's new-found liberty in jeopardy. They fought back, drove the invaders out, and established a bulwark of democracy in Southeast Asia.

Despite the fact that in many countries of Asia, Africa, and Latin America worker organizations are among the strongest national influences on the people and are today producing many leaders of tomorrow, these organizations are plagued by serious problems and are in many cases weak and vulnerable. Many are under the firm control of authoritarian governments. This carries with it the one advantage of usually assuring a reasonably strong financial base, frequently through a compulsory check-off system of dues collection. Those that are not so controlled generally have a very difficult time collecting dues. Few have been able to establish any real collective bargaining relationship with employers. Many are so dependent on political parties that they are scarcely capable of independent action on behalf of their members.

Naturally, the problems and circumstances of labor in the developing countries vary considerably from place to place. The rest of this chapter provides not a complete survey but a sketch of a number of different situations.

Latin America

In Latin America today some two hundred million persons are seeking to ensure their right to life, liberty, and the pursuit of happiness. Sharing much in common with the United States, they nevertheless are painfully conscious of the widening gap between economic conditions in the two Americas. They feel bypassed by the twentieth century, drained of much of their natural wealth, exploited by the industrialist to the north, and, in most places, deprived of the fruits of industrialization. Many countries of Latin America are today hanging in the balance of decision, questioning whether the way of freedom and democracy can meet the appalling needs of their people or whether they must return to some form of the totalitarianism which they have known so often in the past. The trade unions in many countries are the most effective channel through which the people can make known their views on this great decision. In fact it is not too much to say that the future of Latin America will be determined by what direction worker organizations take in the next two or three years.

Worker organizations started in Latin America before World War I in certain key areas: railroads in Argentina; the port workers, sailors, and copper and nitrate miners in Chile; miners and oil workers in Mexico, and textile workers in Brazil and Peru. More recently there has been extensive organization on the plantations of Central America. In their early stages these organizations operated as mutual benefit associations, welfare societies, semifraternal organizations and, above all, agents of nationalism. Reflecting the Marxist-Socialist activities of labor in Europe and responding to the home-grown oppression they found around them, Latin American trade unions soon turned primarily to social protest and resistance against the ruling elites. They openly attacked the exploitative capitalism which for so long had condemned their members to grinding poverty. They insisted on a flood of social legislation which the new governments, dictatorial and otherwise, were eager to enact for self-preservation, whether or not the means for their enforcement and fulfillment existed; and frequently trade unions were ruthlessly suppressed by ruling oligarchies.

On the other hand, trade unionism in Latin America has been weakened almost as much when governments have fallen into the hands of ostensibly pro-labor dictators, such as Perón, Trujillo, and Vargas who reduced unions to nothing more than subservient tools. Like the European Fascists and Communists, these dictators realized early the importance of workers' organizations as a political force and were able to use them effectively as instruments to obtain and preserve vital power. Today, as in Africa and Asia, the trade unions of Latin America are in a life-and-death struggle with communism, but they are also fighting the threat of military dictatorship from the right and the continuing exploitative oligarchy of rich landowners and businessmen. The class struggle is very much alive in Latin American society and it works against collective bargaining. The old European heritage of anarchism, syndicalism and radical socialism is by no means dead. To many Latin American trade unionists, even those who are not Communists, the employer is the enemy; he is to be fought tooth and nail. Mutuality of interest between management and labor is not an easy concept for the Latin American laborer. The differences between rich and poor have been too great for too long, and the ideological vigor of the people is too well developed to expect such notions of cooperation to come easily.

The Latin American worker generally looks to his trade union not primarily to bargain with his employer and to enforce ensuing contract provisions, although it may have that function, but as the defender and promoter of the interests of the working class in the national society. This transcendental role carries the trade union into every phase of national life, foreign and domestic, giving it an overriding political importance.

The Mexican petroleum workers, for example, have been one of the most militant forces in Mexico since the revolution. Their part in the nationalization of the oil industry was decisive. In Mexico, 2.5 million workers, or 70 per cent of the wage earners, belong to trade unions. President López Mateos, former minister of labor, owed his political success largely to the strong backing of labor, and worker organizations help provide important national support for his government. Trade-union representatives account for about one-quarter of the members of the Chamber of Deputies and one-fifth of the Senate in the Mexican Congress.

In Bolivia, labor has unusual political power, being the chief support of the government. Vice President Juan Lechín, who is also head of the mine workers' federation, was one of the two principal figures in the 1952 revolution. Today virtually all nonagricultural workers are organized, and labor leaders have been the principal drafters of plans for nationalization of the mines, agrarian reform, universal suffrage and the participation of labor in the management of certain state enterprises. Bolivian labor, which has traditionally been strongly nationalistic and predominantly socialistic, now appears to be seriously infiltrated with Communists.

The labor movement and its leaders were not ready to assume the great responsibilities they won through their political influence after the revolution. There was a serious lack of managerial talent and the new leaders had little sense of national responsibility. Union chiefs took virtual control of the mines and other industries. If the right forms of technical assistance from the United States had been forthcoming at that crucial time in the country's development, the situation today might well have been much better than it is. While the U.S. government has over the years contributed many millions of dollars to keep Bolivia's economy afloat, these millions have largely gone down the drain, there being no sound structure in the developing society to ensure their effective use.

Trade unions in Brazil have been continually dominated by the government since the Vargas regime of the 1930s and before. By controlling the purse strings of unions, the government until recently has made them ineffectual and apathetic. During the past year or two, however, great changes have taken place. It is unclear at this writing what the final effect will be, but it is certain that the trade unions of Brazil are today an extremely active political force. Having been given new rights and freedoms by former President Quadros, one sector of the Brazilian labor movement is today definitely pro-Communist and the other firmly anti-Communist. The latter met in national conference in São Paulo in July 1961 with 840 delegates, representing more than four million workers. They established a National Trade Union Committee for the Defense of Democracy, which was largely responsible for the failure of the political general strike called by the Communists late in 1961 for the purpose of sweeping Quadros back into power.

The labor movement in Chile, comprising about 15 per cent of the labor force, is of the utmost political importance and is becoming increasingly dominated by Communists and Anarcho-Syndicalists, although the rising influence of the Christian Democratic trade unions is a hopeful factor. Typical of the current situation in Chile and other Latin American countries today is this episode reported from Concepción in the summer of 1961.

> On this Sunday morning, the wide, pleasant walkways along the forested hillsides just half a mile from the city's center were almost deserted—but not quite.

The amplified voice of an impassioned speaker exhorting a crowd of 1500 to carry on the class struggle echoed from the streets, which still showed the scars of last year's earthquake.

In the heart of Concepción, before the ugly gray concrete shell of an unfinished reconstruction project, a rally of steel workers was under way. Speakers denounced both the Government in Santiago for not granting higher wages and the United States Government for "capitalist imperialism."

One labor leader told the assembled workers that theirs was a class struggle and that drastic changes were needed in a do-nothing Government. . . .[4]

In Venezuela, labor is the principal support for the government of Rómulo Betancourt and is a vital element in his critical fight to prevent Communist or military dictatorship in his country. It is significant that even after ten years of repression under the Pérez Jiménez regime, when many worker leaders were imprisoned or exiled, the trade unions were able to stage completely effective general strikes in Caracas and other cities which were instrumental in destroying the dictatorship. Labor's role in the revolution gives it a naturally important place in the politics of today.

The majority of the Venezuelan labor movement is anti-Communist, partially for an interesting and important reason. During the Pérez Jiménez regime the Communists resorted to one of their favorite tactics in Latin America and elsewhere. The party split into two wings, one, the "Red" Communists, opposing the dictatorship, and the other, the "Black" Communists, remaining above ground and cooperating with the regime. Thus when the regime collapsed, the "Black" Communists were in place with power centers throughout the country, while the "Reds," emerging from prison, could claim a place with the new government. This system has often worked surprisingly well elsewhere but the Venezuelans were not fooled by the Communists' hypoc-

[4] Dispatch by Edward C. Burks in *The New York Times,* August 3, 1961.

risy. Although the labor movement had to accept them in coalition, the Communists were excluded from Betancourt's Acción Democrática government.

Venezuela has made great progress in recent years in providing badly needed social reforms and improvements, especially in such areas as taxes, education, housing and land ownership, and cultivation. The trade unions, giving strong support to the government in these efforts, have grown substantially and are today among the most effective and successful labor organizations in the world. Negotiating with large U.S. and European companies in the oil, mining, and machine industries, they have gained collective bargaining contracts equal or superior to those enjoyed by workers in highly industrialized countries. In other industries, they have done equally well negotiating with their own national employers. The major weakness of Venezuela's trade unions is that the leadership layer is very thin. The country's continued growth and independence depends to an important degree on strengthening this leadership and enabling it to withstand growing subversive pressures, both internal and external.

Peru offers another example of a non-Communist labor movement surviving eight years of oppression and purges to emerge a powerful political force. Arturo Sabroso Montoya, an officer of the Peruvian Confederation of Labor and an influential member of the important Aprista party, plays a prominent role in his country and in Latin America generally as an old and vigorous anti-Communist labor leader. Today, however, free labor in Peru is in a life-and-death struggle with Communist forces.

While labor has been a force against dictatorship, it has also been made an instrument of dictators. Juan Perón, it should be remembered, was minister of labor when he came to power in Argentina. He initiated and enforced an impressive body of social legislation, obtaining widespread labor support. He used his office to gain control of the trade unions, which had no inkling of the repression and tragedy which were to follow. After Perón's fall the Argentine trade unions gained their freedom. With more than four million members, about evenly divided between Peronista and non-Peronista elements, they constitute a vital political pressure and played an important part in the events that led to the fall of the Frondizi administration.

Cuba provides a good example of what can happen to labor organizations during a classic Communist take-over. The labor movement in Cuba just prior to Castro's revolution was one of the best organized in Latin America. It had about 1.35 million members of whom 500,000 were in the sugar workers' union. The Cuban Confederation of Workers (CTC) was well financed, benefiting from a dues check-off system, compulsory under national law. Although its leadership was weakened by corruption, the CTC played an important role in international trade-union organizations around the world and was widely regarded as the foremost trade-union federation in Latin America.

During the Castro revolution, the CTC, under the leadership of Eusebio Mujal, maintained an official position of neutrality, which in effect was a position favorable to Batista. Efforts by Castro to initiate general strikes failed twice because the CTC and Cuban Communists refused to support them, although a number of CTC leaders and members were strongly anti-Batista. In opposition to the CTC, Castro then created an underground labor movement under David Salvador, who had been in and out of the Communist party. The international Communist movement and Communists in exile supported Castro, but the Communist party in Cuba and the CTC continued to oppose him.

With the success of the revolution in January of 1959, the CTC leadership was purged. The elected officers in all of the 2,000 local and national unions were deposed and many imprisoned. Provisional officers, loyal to the "26th of July movement," were put in charge under the leadership of David Salvador. They immediately clashed with the Castro Communists in a fight for control. In September 1959, the Communists, with the support of Castro, launched a determined campaign to rid Cuban labor of all non-Communist leaders, including those who were from the "26th of July movement." All who spoke out against the Communists, including David Salvador, were branded as antirevolutionary, pro-Batista, and pro-Mujal. On May 1, 1960, Salvador disappeared and nothing has been heard of him since. Following this, the purge of all non-Communists was swift and complete. Even those who had been closest to Castro in the Sierra Maestra during the early days of the revolution were hunted down, forced into exile, imprisoned, or shot.

Today the trade-union movement in Cuba is a semimilitary labor arm of the Castro regime. The "unions" have succeeded in "persuading" the workers to "vote themselves" wage reductions, extra hours of work without pay, and endless donations of pay to buy arms. They are the core of parades in honor of Castro and are routed out any time a demonstration appears necessary. Cuban labor leaders in exile have bitterly denounced Castro's tyranny and denial of all trade-union rights.

It can thus be seen that in many countries of Latin America, trade unions are of strategic political importance. Except in the more highly industrialized countries, their economic importance is less obvious. There is no doubt that they will continue to press for social justice and improved living and working conditions. There is a question, however, as to what methods will prove most effective. Reliance on the government and legislation for improvement has too often been discouraging, owing principally to the difficulty government has in reforming the entire social system to provide social justice and in reconciling a rising standard of living with national economic development. It is likewise doubtful whether the unions will be satisfied with what they can get for their members solely through collective bargaining.

President Frondizi, speaking to the Conference of the American States Members of the International Labor Organization in Buenos Aires, in April 1961, put the dilemma faced by labor and trade unions this way:

> Within underdeveloped countries, two main factors complicate the problem. On the one hand, there are vested-interest groups which enjoy an economically advantageous position in the present situation of these countries and which refuse to recognize the justice and force of the aspirations of others for a life more in accordance with human dignity. These groups are insensitive to the need for development, or, even worse, are afraid that development would deprive them of their privileges: they can see no other way out than to maintain the *status quo* by overtly or covertly restricting genuine democracy and the expression of the people's will. It is hard to understand the persistence of such attitudes, after the many tragic examples afforded us by contemporary history. On the other hand, it is lamentable to see the error and confusion into which certain sectors of the working population have been led by extremist social agitators. That way lies, for the workers, a struggle foredoomed to failure: the advantages they fight for are unattainable for lack of an adequate economic foundation. The demand for wage increases and better living conditions without corresponding increases in production can only bring about further disturbances in economic activity; these disturbances are reflected mainly in inflationary processes, to the advantage only of privileged groups. Another disturbing factor is the attitude of certain entrepreneur circles, who attempt to improve their position by means of speculation.
>
> Only full development can make effective use of the efforts of all branches of a nation's economy, promote genuine progress and improve the standard of living of all those who have a share in the country's economic life.

In other words, worker organizations find themselves bound to provide benefits for their members in order to maintain their strength and their ability to withstand subversion, but at the same time, they are part of a national effort requiring vast investment in long-term development. The seriousness of the conflict between meeting the demands of workers and the requirements for economic growth make it important to look for some different and untraditional avenues for trade-union action. Otherwise the conflict will be dangerous, either through its effect on development or through the political consequences of frustrating the workers.

Africa

Africa, perhaps even more than Latin America, defies generalization. With this reservation, and by proceeding from one country to another we may, however, find enough in common to justify considering the continent at least in one place in this chapter.

The great bulk of the African population lives within self-sufficient tribal or village economies. Although there is a great deal of shifting about from one place to another among vast, sparsely populated areas, there are islands of development—urban centers, plantations, mining operations, transportation networks—wherein organizations of workers have developed and, despite their economic frailty, have often had a profound effect. These organizations, like their counterparts in Latin America, have been sorely hampered by widespread illiteracy and lack of such rudimentary skills as bookkeeping and typing, if indeed a typewriter were available. African unions also have great difficulty in amassing the income necessary to rent office space, purchase even the simplest equipment such as a bicycle, or support full-time leadership. These handicaps make all the more remarkable the fact that worker organizations have played such highly significant, although in some respects quite different, roles in such countries as Guinea, Ghana, Nigeria, Kenya, Tunisia, Morocco, and the United Arab Republic.

President Nkrumah's successful rise to power in Ghana is due in no small measure to the support which he received from the Ghana labor movement. The trade-union movement started in 1941 when the territory was still the Gold Coast. The British decided to encourage the growth of unions and sent trade unionists to assist in organization. It was no accident that political activity by the new workers' organizations coincided with Nkrumah's formation of the Convention People's Party in 1949. Both the trade unions and the CPP were largely composed of semieducated, detribalized, urban wage and salary earners, most of whom worked in one way or another for the government. Labor and the CPP pressed the British for concessions along the road to independence and in 1950 called a general strike in support of Nkrumah's "Positive Action" program. Nkrumah was jailed together with several trade-union leaders for this activity.

In 1957, independence came and Nkrumah was able to unify the nation behind him, to a considerable degree because of the support he received from the Ghana Trades Union Congress, headed by John Tettegah. Nkrumah soon insisted on firm government control of the TUC both for domestic political reasons and to protect it from Communist subversion via the long arm of the World Federation of Trade Unions, the Communist party's agency in international labor. (At that time the Ghana TUC was firmly allied with the anti-Communist International Confederation of Free Trade Unions.) Ghana trade unions are now firmly in the hands of the ruling party with Tettegah sitting somewhat nervously at Nkrumah's right hand on the Central Committee of the Convention People's Party. But this domination has not meant that the Ghana labor movement has lost importance. In fact, today it is playing a vital role in Ghana's foreign policy as well as serving as a significant internal pro-government force. It was actively associated with the Union Générale des Travailleurs d'Afrique Noire (UGTAN), an indigenous African labor federation with neutralist, anti-Western sentiments. UGTAN has now been replaced by the All-African Trade Union Federation (AATUF). Inspired by the same anti-Western sentiments, the AATUF has become UGTAN's successor as a channel through which Ghana and Guinea are seeking to spread their political influence.

Sekou Touré, President of Guinea, also got his start in politics as a labor leader, standing for a combination of social progress with political independence. It was, indeed, as a labor leader that he first demonstrated his ability to command an almost religious devotion from his followers and became one of the outstanding leaders of the Guinean independence movement. As a result of a sixty-six day strike in 1953 which he led to force a revision of the French African labor code Touré emerged as a political leader. Late in 1956 he became vice president of the *Conseil de Gouvernement,* which made him in effect the premier of Guinea. Touré was clearly the man of the hour, especially among younger, radical elements. After overwhelming electoral victories in 1956 and 1957, Touré and his friends found themselves challenged by a group of students returned from France, labor leaders, and other younger political elements called the Parti du Regroupement Africain, which demanded immediate independence from France. Touré thereupon seized the opportunity presented by the referendum on the new French constitution to order his followers to reject the constitution and thereby secede from France. This fixed Touré's leading position in the independence movement and the new state of Guinea. It was a well-organized labor movement which provided the leverage for such political results.

Tom Mboya's rise to leadership in Kenya and Africa as a whole is also a good example of the new significance of workers' organizations and their leaders. Born on a sisal estate in Kenya's highlands, the son of illiterate parents, he was appointed a Nairobi city sanitary inspector in 1951, but was outraged to find his salary only a fraction of that of a European holding a similar job. He joined the African Staff Association of municipal employees and in 1952 became its president. He converted the association into a union and the same year joined a political group, the Kenya African National Union (KANU). He later became general secretary of the Kenya Federation of Labor. In party, union, and then as chairman of the All-Africa People's Conference at Accra, Mboya has emerged as one of the ablest leaders of the African independence movement.

It is significant that Tettegah, Touré, and Mboya all began their labor-political careers as government workers: as a clerical worker, postal clerk, and sanitary inspector, respectively. This draws attention to the fact that in Africa, government has been, and still is, the largest and most important employer of wage labor. Combining with this the fact that wage and salaried employees of government have had educational advantages far above average and considerable opportunity and capacity for organization, it is easy to see why government worker unions not only form the backbone of the African labor movement but also have a real effect on political developments. These organizations have direct access to government leaders with corresponding influence, which in a fight for independence can be decisive.

In Tunisia, Habib Bourguiba's Neo-Destour party could never have come to power and pressed so successfully for independence and social improvement had it not been for the strong support of organized labor. Similarly, in Morocco, labor emerged as a powerful force in the independence movement. Through its attachments to the masses of the

Moroccan people it has become a vital element in the political situation there today. In a later chapter we will see that the Moroccan federation of labor played an important part in forcing the United States to abandon its air base at Casablanca. Worker organizations have played an important role also in Algeria's freedom movement.

In the Sudan, an agricultural country almost one-third the size of the United States, the transport and communications system is of vital strategic importance. After World War II the railroads, river boats, docks, and hotels, in fact the entire Nile transportation network, were combined into one transportation unit. Its workers became the target of a union-organizing drive by Communists and non-Communists. When it appeared in 1958 that the Communists were gaining control of this powerful complex, the government outlawed union activity. At that time there were 20,000 members in the union and it exerted considerable control over the economic and political development of the country.

Gamal Abdel Nasser was quick to realize the importance of trade unions in his efforts to unify the Arab world and achieve power in the Middle East and Africa. In 1956 when the existing union leadership in various Arab countries was reluctant to cooperate with him, he organized the International Confederation of Arab Trade Unions (ICATU)[5] as an instrument for influencing workers in other Arab and African countries directly from Cairo. He gave the ICATU a handsome building in Cairo and authorized it under his direction to contribute to the unification of Syria and Egypt as well as to encourage, however unsuccessfully, efforts at Arab unity in Tunisia, Libya, Algeria, and Morocco. At the First African Regional Conference of the ILO, held in Lagos in December 1960, the Egyptian workers' delegation was

[5] Later ICATU dropped the "international" from its name and now calls itself merely CATU.

the largest of all present and made strenuous efforts to make common cause with the workers from other African countries, particularly Guinea and Ghana. During the course of the conference, I participated in a radio discussion with Anwar Salama, President of the U.A.R. oil workers' union, one of the ablest Arab trade unionists and a key man in the U.A.R.'s efforts to gain influence and prestige in Africa. He devoted his time during the discussion to persuading his African listeners that the interests of the U.A.R. and Nigeria were, in effect, inseparable.

Within the U.A.R. itself, Nasser has encouraged the growth of strong and vigorous organizations of workers, but the labor movement is entirely dominated by the government. Its purpose is to provide a channel for the worker to assist in bringing the U.A.R. from an underdeveloped to an industrially mature state, and at the same time to help the worker improve his living standards and encourage his enthusiasm for the regime. U.A.R. unions are organized on an industrial basis and have been given the check-off system of dues collection by law. This not only gives them substantial economic strength but gives their members additional benefits because the law provides that 33 per cent of the dues collected must be spent on health facilities or social or professional projects. Workers directly elect their own officers, in local unions and also at higher levels. The law provides, however, that union officers must also be members of the National Union, the single political party of the U.A.R., thus automatically limiting union leadership to supporters of the regime. While this system obviously provides no political independence, it does provide a limited framework for vigorous union activity to improve the working and living conditions of workers as well as contribute to the economic and social development of the country.

With so many political leaders getting their start in the

labor movement—Cyrille Adoula in the Congo is another—
or at least having close ties with it, the relation of unions
to parties and governments has a special significance in
many African countries. But the question is more than one
of personalities or of the ties that unions and parties developed in the struggle for independence. After independence, the new governments find themselves heir to the substantial central power structure established by their colonial
predecessors. They are left in control of key community
services and industries such as railroads, transport, and mining in some countries. Thus the new regimes are, whether
they like it or not, equipped with enormous power and
influence. This concentration of power leads quite naturally
to highly authoritarian practices, but given the problems
of a country like Ghana, a real question arises as to whether
there is any realistic alternative. Given the deep-seated
forces working for disunity, including tribalism and communism, for example, and the almost total lack of education and skills, it would appear that an authoritarian government might be, at least temporarily, unavoidable. It is
to Nigeria's great credit that through the high statesmanship
of its leaders, it has from the beginning avoided the authoritarianism of its neighbors.

The dominant place of government and the close connection of labor leaders with politics make it natural that
trade unions in the new countries should try to solve their
problems more often by appeals for government action than
by collective bargaining. Another reason is that trade unions
in these countries have far less bargaining power with a
private employer than they do with the government. The
former has little interest in workers' votes and opinion
whereas the latter depends on them, at least to some degree.
Other factors also weaken the African union's bargaining
strength with an employer, such as labor surpluses, the low
skill level of workers, the ease of returning to tribal life and

family land, and the union's financial weakness. Also, few colonial regimes left behind a responsible group of local employers, and bargaining with foreign owners is generally too complex for the African trade union.

The governments in turn have felt it necessary to keep a tight rein on trade-union activity or desirable to establish effective political control over the unions. Whether, as the level of education rises and the capacity for democracy develops, the opportunity for its practice will likewise grow is one of the central questions about the future of many African nations. To this process the unions, if they can gain, or keep, a reasonable degree of independence, can make a major contribution.

India

One of the central questions about the role of trade unions in newly developing countries is: Of what importance can a labor union of several thousand men be in a country of many millions which is industrially underdeveloped? India helps provide the answer.

While India has a total population of some 450 million people and a land mass almost half as big as that of the United States, it is a country being led today by an exceedingly small group of men and women. Like the founding fathers of our own country, these are patriots of exceptional intelligence and dedication who are struggling against what often appear to be overwhelming odds. This group of men and women, who literally can be counted in the thousands, are very much a part of India and yet are clearly distinct from the mass of Indian people. They stand out as the only element in Indian society capable of making the tremendous exertion necessary for development.

Assuming that this group of leaders numbers seven or eight thousand, I think it is also probable that those capable

of supporting them in any effective way in the moderniza-
tion of the country, number no more than perhaps seven
or eight million. Remember that about 350 million Indians
live in the more than 600,000 isolated villages, scratching
a meager living from the parched ground and with almost
no contact with the main stream of Indian political and economic life. There are about 100 million more living in urban
centers, of whom perhaps 20 million are employed. Starvation, undernourishment, and a literacy rate of 17 per cent
further reduces the numbers capable of vigorous support
of the leaders.

In the light of these estimates it becomes a little clearer
how an active organization of, say, 200,000 organized workers, under perhaps twenty-five dedicated leaders, can have
a profound and lasting influence. This is especially true if,
as is usually the case, their efforts are directed toward
strategic industries such as steel, coal mining, transportation,
communications, and port operations. Thus a relative handful of people, promising progress toward popular goals, can
be of the utmost political and economic importance. In the
developing countries, numbers are of minor importance
compared to capacity for leadership and ability to organize
behind that leadership.

India's experience throws light on other questions about
the place of labor in underdeveloped countries as well.
There are three principal federations of Indian unions, each
tied to its own political party. The Indian National Trade
Union Congress (INTUC) with about one million members,
grew out of the Ahmedabad Textile Labor Association,
founded some thirty years ago to improve the miserable
conditions in India's textile industry. Gandhi himself
played an important role in its early days, using the Association as a spearhead in his drive for independence. Many of
the present leaders of the Association and INTUC were
close friends of the Mahatma, served jail terms with him,

and practice religiously his creed of nonviolence and peaceful understanding. The chief union in INTUC is still the Ahmedabad Textile Labor Association, which is in many ways a model labor union. Its grievance procedure, community activities, and relations with management would compare favorably with any union anywhere, but it must be said that it is exceptional in Asia. The Association grew with the independence movement and in its early years was largely a political force. After independence, INTUC was formed and continued the close association with the Congress party. Its leaders have alternated between the union and high government posts or positions in Parliament. The present minister of labor, for example, Gulzarilal Nanda, was the former general secretary of the Textile Labor Association, and as such was and is a leading figure in INTUC. Similarly the present general secretary of the Association, Khandubhai Desai, was a former minister of labor.

Following independence, INTUC, like many unions in colonial territories whose leaders had necessarily concentrated on political rather than economic objectives, found itself at loose ends. Its leaders, along with those of the nation as a whole, faced the enormous long-term problems of economic and social development of the country. The role of trade unions in this development was not at all clear. According to Gandhian principles the strike had no place in Indian life, since it was thought of as a manifestation of violence. Perhaps even more important, Congress leaders were determined to succeed with their economic plans and a work stoppage would interfere with that aim. As a result the Indian government has devised a complex body of labor law, requiring compulsory arbitration, which has stifled vigorous collective bargaining and left INTUC uncertain as to its responsibilities and not a little frustrated.

The Communist federation, the All-India Trade Union

Congress (AITUC) with about 600,000 members is, of course, far less frustrated. It is the only existing trade-union federation in India which was started under British rule. During India's struggle for independence, the non-Communist, pro-Gandhi labor leaders were imprisoned. They emerged from jail after independence to find AITUC firmly under Communist control. Directed from Moscow, it has the clear and simple purpose of arousing the masses in protest against their miserable conditions and using every demagogic device to unsettle, divide, and assume increasing control of workers in strategic industries. Unbothered by Gandhi's teachings concerning nonviolence, AITUC does not hesitate to fight if it is in its interest to do so. It is making a particular effort now to gain control of the Indian coal and steel industry which is emerging in the wilderness of Bihar and Orissa within about two hundred miles of Calcutta. There is little question that control of this vital industry and its dependent mining operations would give the Communists a strangle hold on Indian industrial development and could be a powerful political club to hold over her leaders.

The third principal federation of workers in India is the Hind Mazdoor Sabha (HMS), with about 300,000 members, which is tied to the Socialist party. Committed neither to the present Indian administration nor to Moscow, HMS is an aggressive and purposeful federation. It has a number of bright young leaders who have successfully built substantial strength, particularly on the docks in Bombay and Calcutta, which are quite obviously of great strategic importance. In July 1960, HMS led a widespread and bitter strike of government workers which highlighted the Indian government's difficulty in dealing with trade unions. Some nine thousand workers were arrested and many jailed. INTUC played a conspicuous role in recruiting strikebreakers. The strong-arm methods used by the Indian government in suppressing the strike, as well as INTUC's role as a government tool and the general disappointment of the government workers involved, may have helped the cause of the Communists. In addition, INTUC's recent agreement to a Congress party decision to freeze wages for ten years in the interest of economic development will surely be further grist for Moscow's mill.

The links between India's three principal labor federations and the three main political parties are not likely to be broken in the foreseeable future. In India, as in many other Asian and African countries, the trade unions form the most important contact between the political parties and the mass of the people. Their activities reach into every phase of urban life, including politics, housing, hospitals, labor-management relations, public parades and demonstrations, schools and colleges. The collective bargaining function is by no means the most important. Despite this widespread and varied bundle of activities, the place of unions is still vague and often gives rise to conflict. This provides an ideal situation for continuing Communist gains within the labor movement. In India today the Communist labor federation appears to be moving ahead, filling in the widening gaps left by indecision, confusion, and disunity on the part of the two non-Communist federations.

Indonesia

Out of a work force of 35 million persons in Indonesia, more than 5 million are at least nominally members of trade unions. SOBSI, the Communist-led labor federation, has a claimed membership of nearly 3 million. The non-Communists are badly splintered between the KBKI federation with a claimed membership of about a million, and eight or nine other federations totaling together about a million. Indonesia's anti-Western orientation can certainly be laid partially to the need for Indonesian politicians to heed the powerful and unified voice of SOBSI.

In 1945 a revolutionary workers' army was in the forefront of Indonesia's battle for independence. Iwa Kusuma Sumantri, a labor leader who had been exiled by the Dutch and is now president of Padjadjaran University in Bandung, was appointed first minister of social affairs of the Indonesian government. In 1946 the labor unions which had fought so valiantly for freedom combined into the All-Indonesian Central Labor Organization, SOBSI, and led the protest against Dutch "imperialism" and local Dutch entrepreneurs. Soon they were taken over entirely by the Communists. Now SOBSI unions control the work force in most of Indonesia's key industries. As expediency dictates, they have no hesitancy about demanding higher wages and better conditions, regardless of the effect of these demands on the deteriorating economic situation. These "pie-in-the-sky" offerings and demands by SOBSI place the more responsible non-Communist unions, who are supporting the Indonesian government in its efforts to stabilize the economy, in an obviously awkward and vulnerable position. Now and again, as necessary to consolidate its position with the regime, SOBSI will reverse itself and advocate restraint and austerity.

SOBSI's unchecked development obviously represents a serious threat to the continued independence of Indonesia. As in India, other political parties have their own trade-union federations, but the non-Communist groups have failed to unify and organize against SOBSI, which has the largest mass following. There has been, however, in Indonesia one of the most interesting and most important developments in international labor affairs. I shall return to this in later chapters but sketch it here to round out the picture of Indonesia.

The most effective anti-Communist trade union in In-

donesia has been the railway workers' union, known by
the initials PBKA. While this union is to SOBSI about as
David was to Goliath, it has grown remarkably in recent
years and its progress bears close examination. Several
years ago PBKA found itself under severe pressure from
its Communist rival, whose demagogic promises of a better
life were making serious inroads on PBKA's membership.
PBKA wanted to provide real benefits to increase the loyalty
of its members. At the same time the union was dedicated
to the economic development of Indonesia and was unwilling, if not unable, to make irresponsible demands that
would contribute to inflation. With the help of the government it set up a small shop to make shoes and sell them at
low cost to railway workers. Collecting pitifully small sums
from the membership, the union then went on to build a
small rice mill and later a factory for the manufacture of
cheap clothing, all for the benefit of railway workers. PBKA
later received assistance amounting to several hundred
thousand dollars from the U.S. International Cooperation
Administration in the form of technical assistance and used
shoe machinery. These projects were so successful that the
union then started for its members a death benefit program,
a savings and loan association, a consumer cooperative, and
a health and hospitalization program and began working
on plans for a self-help housing program.

These programs have led to a large increase in PBKA's
membership, a great gain in strength in relation to its Communist rival, and nationwide recognition and prestige. More
than that, the enterprises have taught administrative skills
and responsibilities to union leaders and members, ensuring
sound growth and operations in the future. Several factors
were essential to this success. Most important, the union
was guided by the extraordinary leadership of Dr. Kusna
Purardiredja. Second, the plan had the approval and assistance of the government. Third, it probably was more

successful because of the aid ICA contributed. Despite these significant accomplishments PBKA is, of course, still very small indeed beside the well-organized, well-financed, and widespread organization the Communists have in SOBSI. But the experience both gives point to some questions and suggests some answers.

Key Questions and Some Possible Answers

This rapid review of the position and problems of organized labor in a number of underdeveloped countries has suggested some of the questions Americans must ask themselves as part of the process of devising more effective policies concerned with the position of labor in underdeveloped countries. It has also indicated at least the beginnings of answers.

In most new countries, workers' organizations have been important in the struggle for independence. Ties with parties and governments have become close. After independence, new governments feel it necessary to maintain strict controls over trade-union movements for political as well as economic reasons. This restricts the independence of unions but in too many cases does not exclude Communist infiltration. How long is this situation likely to persist? Should the United States be concerned whether unions develop a higher degree of independence? Can it, and should it, try to influence the process?

In virtually all of the countries of the developing world the Communists are either gaining or holding their own in their efforts to control organizations of workers. It is quite clear that the role of Communist-led unions in these countries is to disrupt, sow dissension and dissatisfaction with the status quo, and prepare the ground for subversion and overthrow. What then is the role of the non-Communist trade union?

Is it merely to increase wages and improve working conditions? Is this a practical role, given the necessity in many of these countries to reinvest every spare penny in new development? Is traditional, Western-style collective bargaining practical in underdeveloped countries or should labor's primary aim be to influence the government?

Invariably the non-Communist labor organizations are plagued by a variety of problems in maintaining the loyalty of their members and their own intrinsic strength. For a variety of reasons collective bargaining, resulting in wage increases or improvement in conditions, is impractical in many countries. The union's attachment to a political party seems as a practical matter to have the result that the union suffers with the party, but rarely prospers with it. The Communist-led unions to a considerable degree escape from these inhibitions and so have a good chance to gain strength.

From our review one rather unusual example shines forth: the case of the railroad workers in Indonesia. Perceiving that there is more than one way to skin a cat, PBKA itself engaged in activities which would meet some of the urgent needs of its membership for food, clothes, and other necessities of life. In the process it strengthened itself organizationally. Is the same technique more widely applicable? Could INTUC, for example, solve its dilemma of meeting the needs of its members and at the same time remaining loyal to the austerity program of the Indian government by engaging in comparable projects?

Could the United States help encourage this kind of development? We put hundreds of millions of dollars at the disposal of governments for their use in developing their countries. Should we also give help directly to nongovernmental institutions, such as trade unions, which are promoting the principles of liberty and social justice in which we believe? In thinking of an answer to this question, we should remember that the little assistance which we gave

PBKA was haphazard and remains one of the very few contributions we have made to a venture of this sort. We should also remember that in Indonesia alone there are at least six other independent, non-Communist unions which might be encouraged to do the same thing and which have among their leaders men with the education and leadership capacity to do it successfully.

While the situations are not fully comparable, experience in Tunisia, Lebanon, and Israel suggests that we need a broader perspective of the possible role of unions than we would get from looking only at the familiar scenes of North America and Western Europe.

The Union Générale Tunisienne du Travail (UGTT), played a dominant role in Bourguiba's fight for Tunisian independence in 1954 and before. It has continued to have great influence since independence. At least four leading trade unionists have become members of the cabinet. This influence has made the UGTT a prime target for Communist infiltration. Nasser has sought to influence it through ICATU (later CATU). Neither the Communists nor Nasser have yet been successful, and today UGTT stands as possibly the strongest organization of workers on the continent of Africa with great influence south as well as north of the Sahara.

Traditionalists will argue that the UGTT is not a "free trade union" because it is dominated by the government. So it is. Yet within the governmental framework there is no question about its strength or its effectiveness, about the services it is providing its members, or about its importance in Africa today and in the future. It is certainly free in the sense that it is not dominated by a foreign power and free in the sense that it has a real influence in the development of Tunisia; and the day may be soon approaching when the government will need the UGTT more than the UGTT now needs the government.

How has the UGTT maintained and increased its strength and provided benefits to its members, despite the urgent demands for national economic development in Tunisia? Membership has risen from 80,000 in 1954 at the time of independence to more than 220,000 today. How has UGTT insulated itself against the letdown which normally afflicts worker organizations in former colonial areas after the glorious and heroic fight for independence has been won? How has it kept itself strongly anti-Communist in the midst of the neutralist sentiments of the Arab world?

One answer to these questions certainly is the strong emphasis which the UGTT has placed upon cooperatives. Its Deputy Secretary General, Habib Tliba, is in charge of the UGTT "union of cooperatives." The union operates its own plant, with two hundred employees, making clothing which is sold through a union retail outlet in Tunis for 15 per cent to 20 per cent less than commercial competitors. UGTT owns three fishing trawlers which bring their catch to the city of Sfax, from which it is taken by union trucks to Tunis. The trawlers, trucks, and docks all have refrigeration units, something hitherto unknown in Tunisia. Again, UGTT undersells commercial fishing operators. During the last three years the union has built and sold about nine hundred houses to union members on land contributed by the government. By making a very small down payment and small monthly contributions, a worker can own his home in twenty years. The UGTT is now manufacturing hardware and furniture as well. The union is also operating a printing plant, its own bus service, retail grocery stores, and a bakery. It has set up a kerosene cooperative and is training displaced cart drivers to drive trucks. In 1960, 2,400 persons were employed by UGTT cooperatives.

All this has been done, it should be noted, without any assistance whatsoever from ICA or the U.S. government. Now, however, the union has requested some assistance in training managerial personnel, bookkeepers, and administrators for their cooperatives.

In Lebanon in 1956 the Communists had made severe inroads among the hotel and restaurant workers, a union of considerable influence and political importance in that country. The union split into two factions, and with ICA assistance, the non-Communist group was equipped with modest medical clinics. It set up health centers in Beirut and Tripoli which has weakened considerably the Communist rival.

Perhaps the classic prototype for a union directly participating in economic and social development as well as serving as a bargaining agent is the General Federation of Jewish Labor in Israel (Histadrut). It is not too much to say that today in Israel, Histadrut even rivals the state in economic and political importance. Ninety per cent of Israel's wage earners are members of Histadrut. It has not only regularly raised their standards of living through wage increases and improved working conditions, but has provided them with housing, vocational training, hospitals, health insurance, and countless other benefits. Apart from the government, it is the largest single employer in Israel, employing nearly thirty thousand workers. Furthermore, Histadrut has construction projects under way in many countries of Asia and Africa. It built Ghana's port, Sierra Leone's parliament building, housing developments in Addis Ababa, and airports in Somalia and Turkey. It has a substantial say in the determination of the economic policies and plans of Israel. Some say it even dominates them. It runs the Afro-Asian Institute for Labor Studies and Cooperation, which every six months teaches some seventy Africans and Asians how Histadrut and Israel achieved their phenomenal development. I have seen this Institute in operation and there is no question that the Israeli example is extremely compelling to those who face many of the same problems which Israel faced a scant ten years ago, such as making the desert bloom, industrializing rapidly, training for industrialization, and intensifying agricultural production. It is not by chance that immediately after Ghana achieved independence John Tettegah visited Israel to see Histadrut in action.

Of course, Histadrut is a special case. It was founded in 1920, preceding the State of Israel by twenty-six years. Its aims were social justice and equality, and it set about to cope with the many problems confronted by the early Jewish settlers in Palestine.[6] It promoted land settlement through cooperative villages. It trained immigrants for manual work and set up economic enterprises to provide employment. It established mutual aid funds, hospitals, and schools. At the same time it established a network of labor unions, many of which came to be bargaining agents with the operating division of Histadrut itself. Gradually it grew until today it is the largest construction company in Israel and carries on a myriad of other entrepreneurial operations. At the same time the benefits and services which it provides have in many cases been extended to the entire population.

Histadrut without doubt is one of the most important arms of Israeli foreign policy. Not only do its construction operations take it all over the world, but its example as a trade union is attracting ever increasing attention from worker leaders in Africa and Asia, particularly those who having won independence are somewhat at a loss as to how to proceed next. Conscious of their political importance, realizing their vulnerability to subversion and overthrow, and

---

[6] First Histadrut policy statement, made in 1920: "The Histadrut considers it its duty to create a new type of Jewish worker, and to see to it that while settlement is being fostered, the Jewish worker who comes into being as a result of this very process, shall be assured the place he deserves. The Histadrut includes all workers who live by their own labor without exploiting the labor of others; it regulates all matters concerning the working class in the fields of trade union activities, settlement, and education, with the aim of building a Jewish workers' community in Palestine."

desirous of building some measure of independent strength into their organizations, they are looking more and more at Israel and Tunisia. For in these two countries it has been clearly demonstrated that a trade union can indeed improve the welfare of its members and at the same time advance the total economic and social development of the nation.

Chapter III

THE COMMUNIST CHALLENGE
AND FREE LABOR'S RESPONSE

Since the October Revolution, the subversion and control of trade unions has been part of the international Communist conspiracy. As the trade unions of Africa, Asia, and Latin America have increased in importance and gained strategic influence on the political as well as the economic development of these areas, communism has increased its efforts to control them. Leaders of the non-Communist world and its labor movements would be deluding themselves if they failed to recognize that Moscow and Peking are having considerable success in these efforts.

Aided and inspired by Fidel Castro and his most significant export, *Fidelismo,* Communist leaders are now exerting serious pressures on the workers' organizations of Venezuela, Bolivia, Chile, Ecuador, Peru, and Brazil, among others. As a result, the freedom of these countries is in jeopardy. Across the South Atlantic and especially in Guinea and Ghana, the Communists are seeking to divide African labor and break its ties of friendship with free labor movements. And in Asia they have gained substantial influence within vital trade-union groups, controlling strategic elements of the economy in India and, even more dramatically, in Indonesia. Also, in Ceylon, Communist (in this case Trotskyite) efforts among dock workers at Colombo kept that vital port virtually inoperable for close to two years.

Indeed it is not too much to say that in many of the newly developing countries, the Communists have been more successful in the trade unions than through the Communist parties themselves. Of course, in any given country the dividing line between what is done by the party and the action of a Communist-dominated trade union may be slight, but where a distinction can be made, the latter has often had more impact.

Large numbers of young worker leaders are taken to Moscow, Peking, Budapest, and East Berlin each year for training and indoctrination. For example, in 1959 and 1960, thirty labor delegations from Africa, composed of from four to ten persons each, visited Communist-bloc countries, compared to a total of fifty individual African labor leaders who visited the United States in the same period.

At the same time, no more potent anti-Communist force exists throughout the less-developed world than worker organizations. They are the first targets and thus the first line of defense. We can remember well that in our own country, immediately following World War II, when Senator McCarthy was still just another marine veteran, the American labor movement was already actively ridding itself of Communists. Perhaps most memorable were the battles among the automobile workers during and after World War II which ended with the defeat of the Communists in 1947, and later the struggle within the electrical workers' union. Secretary of Labor Arthur Goldberg deserves special praise for his successful efforts to rid the CIO of Communists in those days. We can also well remember that when Chairman Khrushchev came to the United States in 1960 perhaps his most unpleasant evening was spent with leaders of American labor in San Francisco. Men whom he had called the exploited tools of Wall Street asked him questions he could not answer. He was driven to mumbling repeatedly that Walter Reuther was a "lackey of the capitalists," a charge which was ridiculous to millions around the world.

The American labor movement is now joined with its brother organizations around the free world, seeking to help workers in newly developing countries build strong trade unions, capable of advancing the welfare of workers and withstanding the pressures of communism from without or dictatorship within.

On the Communist side of this battle is the World Federation of Trade Unions, probably the most effective of the Communist front organizations at work in the world today. The WFTU is composed of Communist trade unions in the Sino-Soviet bloc, France (CGT), Italy (CGIL), and in the developing world, most importantly Indonesia and India. It claims a membership of 102 million workers. Its program is almost entirely directed at the free world. It has virtually no program or interest in the workers in the Sino-Soviet bloc where more than 90 per cent of its members live and work. While the WFTU is the most important single Communist agency concerned with international labor, individual Sino-Soviet bloc countries carry on a variety of political, cultural, informational, and conspiratorial campaigns day after day around the world, directed largely at workers and their organizations.

On the free world side, the most important international organization is the International Confederation of Free Trade Unions, founded in 1949 when all non-Communist organizations left the WFTU. It claims a membership of 57 million in more than 100 countries. About one-fourth of the total is accounted for by United States unions. European unions provide about 40 per cent of the membership, Latin American 13 per cent, Asian and Australian 12 per cent,

African 3 per cent, and Canadian about 5 per cent. The ICFTU is dedicated to improving the welfare of workers generally and strengthening non-Communist trade unions against subversion by the WFTU.

Another important non-Communist international organization of trade unions is the International Federation of Christian Trade Unions which has some 2 million members with influence primarily among Christian trade unions in Europe, Viet-Nam, and some of the former colonies of France and Belgium in Africa. The IFCTU also has some strength in Chile, as well as in a few other Latin American countries.

Of increasing importance are the nineteen International Trade Secretariats. These are international federations of national trade unions operating in the same or related trades or industries. They cooperate with and are dependent for some financial assistance on the ICFTU, but are independent in their operations. In spite of recent emphasis by the Secretariats on regional activities in the less-developed world, they are still composed principally of European and North American trade unions. The nineteen Secretariats have an affiliated membership of approximately 35 million, of which roughly 64 per cent is in Europe, 24.6 per cent in the Western Hemisphere, 10 per cent in Asia, and .8 per cent in Africa. Nearly forty American unions belong to seventeen Secretariats.

The World Federation of Trade Unions

The sole aim of the WFTU is to promote the cause of the Communist party around the world. It is a tool of the party, financed, organized, and staffed by the party. It will adopt any tactic, any policy, any principles that will advance the party's interests. It will wear any mask the play requires, and it has no hesitation about changing faces between acts. As we saw, in Venezuela the WFTU cooperated with both Pérez Jiménez and the revolutionaries. In India, it was on the side of maharajas and of landless peasants. In French West Africa it was identified with colonial French unions as well as anticolonial independence fighters. Sometimes it gets caught and loses ground but often it gets away with its clever subterfuges. The WFTU is, in short, a formidable foe, especially for those who are governed by principles and for whom consistency and honesty are virtues.

The hypocrisy of the WFTU is perhaps best illustrated by the obvious differences between 95 per cent of its affiliates, the trade unions of the Sino-Soviet bloc, and its affiliates and preachments in and to the outside world. A trade union in any of the bloc countries is used by the state and the party to carry out administrative services. It is in no sense regarded as the representative of the workers, as a channel for grievances, or as a means for improvement of conditions. According to the Soviet Trade Union Statute of 1954:

> The trade unions organize socialist emulation [or, as it is sometimes translated, "competition"] of workers and other employees to raise labor productivity to the utmost, to fulfill and overfulfill state plans . . . to improve quality and reduce production costs, to make full use of all the reserves of the socialist economy. . . .[1]

János Kádár, the infamous puppet prime minister of Hungary, said: "In the Bolshevik system, trade unions have become transmission belts: their role is restricted to the in-

---

[1] Quoted in International Labor Office, *Trade Union Rights in the U.S.S.R.*, Studies and Reports, New Series, No. 49 (Geneva: Author, 1959), Appendix II, p. 86. Most quotations in this and other chapters that are not footnoted, such as those from WFTU, ICFTU, and ILO meetings, are drawn from published proceedings and other reports. Some statements and facts are taken from unclassified but unpublished papers available to me when I was in the Department of Labor.

tensification of production, the organization and popularization of work competition, the affirmation of the leadership of the Party. . . ." Obviously in 1956 there were some workers in Budapest who did not agree with him.

Trud, the official organ of Bulgarian trade unions, expressed it as follows:

> Under popular democracy the situation and role of the working class has radically changed and consequently the role and situation of the trade unions has changed too. Today the working class is the leading power in the country. . . . It is the proletarian State itself that looks after the interests of the workers; thus the trade unions have become the mainstays of the Party in strengthening the regime.

Quite clearly under such a system there is theoretically no cause for the strike because in theory the workers own everything and run the state. Any attempt at a strike would thus of course be considered "counterrevolutionary" and ruthlessly quelled. Probably no aspect of Communist doctrine has less appeal in the non-Communist world than this one. None is more representative of everything the emerging countries have been fighting to abolish. None is more unfree, dictatorial, and repressive. So quite naturally the WFTU is scrupulous in its silence about this doctrine abroad.

The Communists realize full well that the aims and objectives of free trade unions are far more appealing than those of their own; so without the slightest hesitation they have, for propaganda purposes, adopted the language of free labor as their own and proclaimed "a united front" with all who are seeking to improve the welfare of workers. In 1960 the WFTU, meeting in Peking, issued a statement declaring its goals to be: general wage increases and a minimum guaranteed wage, equal pay for equal work, the elimination of all forms of discrimination, reduction in the cost of living, free access to vocational training, shorter hours, longer holidays, improved safety measures, protection against unemployment, abolition of forced labor, social security improvements, and many more. That these objectives had no conceivable bearing on, or relation to, the vast majority of its membership in the Communist bloc was of no concern whatsoever. The purpose of this statement was purely and simply to make the WFTU and its leaders more acceptable to the trade-union leaders of Asia, Africa, and Latin America; to convince them that the WFTU was eager to make common cause with them and welcome to its breast any and all who believed in these principles; to give the impression that the WFTU was not fighting the cold war or extending "East-West conflict" but was pleading for the opportunity to join with all organizations in securing social justice. What the statement did not say, of course, was that if by chance these aims were accomplished and the target country were to fall within the orbit of Moscow, all these aspirations would go out the window, and the "comrades" in the trade unions would be the first to find themselves in prison or exile.

The WFTU is making continuous efforts to persuade the ICFTU, its affiliates, and the IFCTU to join in its "united front." In Africa it seeks to forge unity by attacking colonialism, imperialism, and racial discrimination. In Latin America it rails against United States "capitalism" and American corporations for "stealing the wealth of the Americas." It seeks to make common cause with the Confederation of Arab Trade Unions, and it invites any and all to its world congresses.

While actual affiliation with and membership in the WFTU is slight compared to that of the ICFTU in Asia, Africa, and Latin America, the growing degree of collaboration is alarming. At the Fourth World Congress of the WFTU in Leipzig in 1957, there were 181 Afro-Asian delegates from nineteen affiliated and nineteen unaffiliated organizations. Among the latter, two belonged to the ICFTU, one belonged to an anti-Communist International Trade Secretariat, and one was about to join the ICFTU. Sekou Touré was there as leader of the anti-Western General Union of Black Africa (UGTAN). At the Leipzig congress the WFTU presented an invitation to all when it declared: "The World Trade Union Congress shall be open to all trade union organizations and their participation shall not imply their affiliation with the WFTU." Observers were included in the roll call with members and were permitted to vote.

Such honeyed treatment has drawn non-Communist trade union representation from all over the world, despite the strict orders of the ICFTU to the contrary. Non-Communists from India, Australia, Chile, and other countries now regularly attend May Day ceremonies in Peking or Moscow, anniversaries of the October Revolution, and international conferences of all sorts. Typical of the WFTU's all-embracing "united front" technique was the Pacific Coast and Asian Dockers' Conference in Tokyo in May 1959. Engineered by the WFTU, it was cosponsored by the non-Communist but anti-Western Japanese Dock Workers' Union and Harry Bridges' U.S. Longshoremen's and Warehousemen's Union, notorious for its Communist leanings.

Similar conferences of non-Communist and Communist trade unions are surely being planned to discuss such issues as U.S. relations with Cuba, racial discrimination, and colonialism. In these and other forums the WFTU can take advantage of the new "solidarity" movements which are attaining tremendous political force—Africa for the Africans, Asia for the Asians, Cuba, Si, Yanqui, No, etc. It identifies itself with movements which suit its purposes at the time. It merges its Communist affiliates with non-Communist unions with the hope of controlling the latter. It wiggles and twists its way, conforming opportunistically to current power situations, never failing, however, to keep its over-all objective clearly in mind.

For example, in 1959 Louis Saillant, Secretary General of the WFTU, teaching at the organization's school in Budapest, told his African students that the nationalism which they were espousing was merely another form of the class struggle, that their fight was the Communists' fight, and that their effort to secure independence was inseparably linked to the world-wide class struggle. The appeal of the WFTU can be seen by the resolutions of its General Council at Peking in June 1960 which spoke of the organization's "increasingly effective support to the workers and their organisations in the countries fighting colonialism, irrespective of their international affiliation." The Council called on unions to come together in "an International Trade Union Committee for Solidarity with the Workers and Peoples of South Africa," in order to "give the maximum effective support" to "the fight against apartheid in South Africa. . . ." It also suggested "the possibility of publishing an African trade union information bulletin to carry news of the struggles of the African trade unions against colonialism and for a better life."

Given the finances at its disposal, the large number of trained organizers it has in the field, the length of time during which it has been at work, and its undoubted utopian appeal to unsophisticated peoples, it is surprising and encouraging that the Communist labor effort has not been more successful in Africa, Latin America, and Asia.

In Africa, communism has as yet found little support, and the great majority of African unions are led by non-Communists, who, in many cases are articulate anti-Communists. The Communists and the WFTU have thus been forced to adopt an interim policy of encouraging African worker organizations to remain "neutral" and not to affiliate with any international organization. With this end in view they are attacking European and U.S. labor movements as "agents of colonialism," exploiting nationalist fervor among African leaders. They are seeking to build the remains of Sekou Touré's neutralist UGTAN into a larger and more influential All-African Trade Union Federation (AATUF). The first preparatory conference for such a federation was held in Accra in 1959 when it became apparent that UGTAN was not becoming the useful tool that Communists had intended it to be. There is no doubt that the WFTU tried hard to make UGTAN an instrument for subversion, because Abdoulaye Diallo, a former WFTU vice president, was made a leading UGTAN official. He was also Guinean minister in Ghana, incidentally, and undoubtedly played a role in securing the withdrawal of the Ghana Trades Union Congress from the ICFTU in 1959.

A group of WFTU-trained African trade unionists are now working to build a strong AATUF which will require its members to renounce affiliation with any international trade-union organization. At a conference in Casablanca in June 1961, it was plain, however, that African labor is sorely divided on this issue. John Tettegah of Ghana and Seydou Diallo of Guinea, both bitterly hostile to the ICFTU, supported the WFTU nonaffiliation line. Tom Mboya of Kenya, a vice president of the ICFTU, and Lawrence Borha, the outstanding trade-union leader of Nigeria, favored an AATUF, but argued that members of the federation should be able to retain their existing affiliations if they so desired. Ahmed Tlili of Tunisia urged that the question of disaffiliation be postponed. The moderates, Mboya, Borha, and Tlili, boycotted the final session and in their absence the chairman of the conference took it as decided that the AATUF would not be affiliated with any other international organization and that individual members of the new body would have to sever existing links within ten months. There will undoubtedly be continuing friction and it seems doubtful that we have heard the last of this issue. Tlili returned to Tunis, complaining that the majority of the conference delegates were fellow-travelers, including Africans who had lost all contact with African workers and were living abroad in Communist countries. Borha delivered this parting shot: "Those who shout at the top of their voices for positive neutrality do not say that when they leave this hall they will not go to Moscow." [2] And Mboya challenged those responsible for distributing a forged document slandering the ICFTU to come into the open and defend it. In January 1962, Tlili, Mboya, and the leaders of Senegalese labor played key roles in setting up the African Trade Union Confederation (ATUC) at a conference in Dakar. The new organization was based on the principle rejected at Casablanca that each member union shall be free to choose for itself whether it will be affiliated with ICFTU or IFCTU.

By encouraging African unions to remain "neutral" and unaffiliated with the ICFTU, the WFTU hopes to isolate these organizations so that Communist groups, working from within, may have an unobstructed path to subversion and overthrow.

Much the same tactic is being employed in Latin America. There the Communists are seeking to exclude the United States from contact with Latin American worker organizations and to merge Communist with non-Communist labor groups. The WFTU has decided to disband its ineffectual regional organization, the Confederation of Latin American Workers (CTAL), and bring pressure on the ICFTU to dissolve its regional arm, the Inter-American Regional Organization of Workers (ORIT). In giving up CTAL, the Communists would not be losing much because it has very little stature in Latin America and few affiliates. ORIT, on the other hand, has a considerable structure in many countries and provides important assistance to non-Communist labor.

[2] *AFL-CIO Free Trade Union News,* June 1961, p. 6.

By isolating Latin American labor from the United States, the Communists would get a free hand to work from within Latin American trade unions, where they have substantial strength. They would be able to carry forward unchecked their so-called unity drive with the objective of pulling all Latin American organizations under the Communist tent.

Their tactics were described vividly and with some desperation by a high-ranking Brazilian trade-union leader in a private letter:

The infiltration of trade unions is increasing substantially every day. The tactics used continue to be the same, with the addition, at this point, of exploitation of Party policy. The objectives of this infiltration are clear: to establish a strong foundation in the trade unions, and then to proceed with the establishment of "single" bodies, consisting of a single national central organization and state central organizations affiliated with the national. The method of activating the workers includes two types of appeals: subjects of a political and economic nature, both national and international, and the immediate demands of the workers, such as legislation of concern to labor: minimum wage, social security, right to strike, etc. This is set against a background of propaganda about large-scale economic exploitation by the United States, which they try to whip up by means of fake nationalism. Meanwhile, inside the unions, they wage a hard fight against the leaders who oppose this program, setting up wage commissions consisting almost entirely of leftists, which try, by means of absurd demands, to make the leaders unpopular with the membership, so as to get rid of them in the next election. Besides, they employ a sort of internal purge; when they succeed in taking over the leadership of the organization, they get rid of the opposition by the tactic of excusing them from paying monthly union dues; and when their dues are found to be in arrears, they are expelled. The lack of understanding and the suspicion of many bosses also are duly exploited by means of liberal contributions or by stirring up disrespect for the authority of the union leaders in their field.

The note on which they hammered without letup was "the interference of foreign organizations in our country," a very praiseworthy attitude if it had been sincere; and it should have called for at least an explanation on our part, since apparently the fact of our membership in an organization does not imply that it can interfere in the internal activity of its members. But actually the purpose was to put pressure on the Confederations to make them withdraw from the two internationals, so that the municipal and state organizations could affiliate directly with the international union organizations whose statutes permit such affiliation; in other words, the whole procedure was aimed at driving the Confederations away from the ICFTU and the ORIT—which are democratic organizations and therefore opposed to Communism—so that the unions and federations could join the international Communist organizations.

In Asia, the influence of the All-China Federation of Trade Unions (ACFTU) is so great that the Communists have almost limitless capacity for subversion and control through labor. In 1957, the ACFTU sent 149 delegations comprising 900 members to 28 different countries and there is no reason to suppose that this effort has not been increased since then. The Indonesian labor movement, dominated as we have seen by the Communist SOBSI, is a perfect example of how successful Communist control has become. In that country there is little need for "united front" propaganda because the opposition is not important enough for the Communists to worry about.

In India, in contrast, Communist leaders of the All-India Trade Union Congress, financed heavily by Moscow, have for some time spoken of the necessity of a united front with non-Communist labor groups. But increasingly, as AITUC has grown stronger its main effort has been to expand its influence, subvert the opposition, and gain control of vital areas of the Indian economy.

Red China's growing influence in Japan through Japanese labor is another alarming example of effective subversion. The largest labor federation of Japan, known as SOHYO, is dominated by left-wing and sometimes pro-Communist Socialists. In 1960 it received a substantial sum from the U.S.S.R., Communist China, and other bloc countries in support of a coal miners' strike. SOHYO played an important role in organizing the vigorous protest against the Japanese-U.S. Security Treaty and the visit of former President Eisenhower.

Three factors have contributed to Communist successes:

1. *Flexibility.* The WFTU does not insist on affiliation. It will give help to anyone who wants it if Moscow's general purposes would be served. If the WFTU is unacceptable, local Communist organizers move in and work from within key organizations. If the non-Communist movements are strong, a plea is made for unity, and often the Communists will, with a show of magnanimity, dissolve their organization and merge with their non-Communist "brothers." If you can't lick them, join them, Moscow says, and once having joined them, lick them from within. If, on the other hand, the Communist organization is as strong or stronger than the opposition, an all-out offensive to obliterate the competition is undertaken. Hypocritical, shifty, opportunistic, the Communists are prepared to use any trick that will work. Power, regardless of principle, is the objective.

2. *Financial support.* The WFTU and other Communist labor groups receive funds, training, and close support of all sorts from Sino-Soviet bloc countries, especially the U.S.S.R. and China. This money, of course, is state money, not the dues of union members. It comes fast when it is needed and its expenditure is clearly connected and coordinated with the fulfillment of over-all Communist foreign policy. Its expenditure does not have to be debated, voted, accounted for democratically, or publicly announced.

3. *Opportunism,* and the ability to take advantage of basic moving forces. The Communists ride, however hypocritically, the wave of anticolonialism and nationalism, appealing to the pride of rising nations and urging them to cast off the political and economic ties which they have known for so long.

Put all together, this adds up to a potent offensive combination. But it has a basic flaw. It is fundamentally dishonest. Like a rusty nail beneath a painted surface, the truth comes through and the leaders of the new world catch a glimpse of it from time to time before it is painted over again. In international forums, such as the International Labor Organization and the United Nations, they see the frenzied efforts of the Communists to hide the truth or twist it. They see the ruthless oppression that has accompanied all attempts to raise the flag of liberty in a Communist country. They see, perhaps dimly, the threat of a new and more dreadful colonialism than they ever knew before. They sense the yawning gap between what is preached and what is practiced.

We should never conclude that the leaders of Africa and Asia are primitive men, easily fooled or led like sheep. Quite to the contrary, for the most part they frequently see with clearer eyes than we. They have been tested in the terrible trials of revolution and national birth. Young in years, they are old in experience. In most cases, they are shrewd, intelligent, sophisticated, and year by year, as they see the world around them unfold and catch recurring glimpses of the truth, they are becoming more so. In this sense, time is against the Communists. For as time goes by the core of their doctrine will show through more and more. The leaders of Latin America will know that what is told them is quite different from what is practiced in Asia. The leaders of Africa will see that what they have been promised is not what the Cubans got. And all will see that their earnest pleas for peace, for liberty, for help, for the conversion of the gun into the ploughshare are being callously neglected by those who pretend to heed them most.

This is the hope of freedom, for free peoples, whether they like it or not, must be honest about themselves. They cannot hide the truth. Our bad is plain for all to see beside our good. We cannot wear false faces long, for we ourselves rip off the mask of deceit as soon as we discover it. Our enemies cannot expose themselves, even though they may want to, for it would mean suicide.

So it is that the labor movements of the free world meet the Communist offensive armed with a powerful weapon— the truth. This is not to say the leaders of these movements always use that weapon or always even know where it is. But it is at their disposal if they will see it; and it is not and cannot be in the arsenal of their adversaries.

The International Confederation of Free Trade Unions

Following World War II most of the major trade-union organizations of the world, Communist and non-Communist, belonged to the World Federation of Trade Unions. United States labor was represented in the WFTU by the Congress of Industrial Organizations (CIO), but the American Federation of Labor (AFL) refused to join, being unwilling, even in 1945, to regard Communist trade unions as anything but agents of the state, and communism as anything but an imperialist revolution bent on world domination. Other trade unions of the free world were eager to keep the World War II alliance together and promote trade-union solidarity against the evils of fascism for the benefit of all workers everywhere. Gradually they became convinced, however, that the Communist form of dictatorship made dishonest the Soviet Union's claim to have workers' organizations independent of government. When the U.S.S.R. attempted to press its opposition to the Marshall Plan upon the unions of Western Europe, all but the outright Communists rebelled, and in 1949 the WFTU broke apart. The non-Communist trade unions, meeting in London, established the International Confederation of Free Trade Unions which was from the start what it is today, a loose combination of independent affiliates bound together by a desire to encourage the growth of free trade unions and reject the Communist system.

The first general secretary of the ICFTU was J. H. Oldenbroek. As leader of the International Transport Workers' Federation, one of the most powerful of the Trade Secretariats, Oldenbroek had shown himself to be a vigorous anti-Communist and had successfully resisted WFTU efforts to integrate all the Trade Secretariats under its organization. When Communist unions sought to sabotage U.S. efforts to rehabilitate Europe by refusing to unload Marshall Plan goods at the docks, Oldenbroek and the Transport Workers' Federation, with substantial help from American railway and other unions, organized vigilante committees which ensured safe and speedy unloading along the European coastline.

The American Federation of Labor, joining the new ICFTU with much prestige for having seen the truth about communism before most, wholeheartedly endorsed Oldenbroek's election; but by 1955 American labor was in the forefront of a drive to get rid of him. Dissatisfied with the slow progress being made in organizing industrial and agricultural workers in Asia, Africa, and Latin America into strong, democratic organizations, AFL leaders moved for a change. Later they were joined by leaders of the CIO.[3] At first, most European trade unionists remained loyal to their

[3] John P. Windmuller, *American Labor and the International Labor Movement, 1940 to 1953*, No. 2 of *Cornell International Industrial and Labor Relations Reports* (Ithaca: Cornell University, 1954).

colleague. They felt he was doing the best job he could in difficult circumstances, but American labor's aggressive and tenacious insistence on his removal was too much to resist. In 1960 Omer Becu, who had succeeded Oldenbroek as general secretary of the Transport Workers' Federation and had been president of the ICFTU for several years during the fifties, took over as general secretary of the organization. This long and often bitter struggle over the leadership was only one example of the dissension which has characterized much of the ICFTU's history.

ICFTU membership figures appear impressive. In 1960 it claimed as affiliates 135 organizations in more than 100 countries with some 57 million members, compared to 67 organizations in 51 countries with 48 million members in 1949.[4] The vast majority of worker organizations in developing countries are affiliated with the ICFTU. Notable exceptions include: Communist federations in Indonesia, India, and Cuba; some Arab unions, affiliated with the neutralist Confederation of Arab Trade Unions; and other neutralist or anti-Western organizations in Burma, Ghana, Guinea, Union of South Africa, Argentina, Bolivia, and Chile, which are unaffiliated internationally. The extent and breadth of membership has posed many policy problems for the ICFTU. While it is still financed largely by American and Western European contributions, its new membership from the less-developed countries is forcing reconsideration of its organization, purposes, and operations. For example, Europe and North America, which in 1949 had a clear majority of the votes on the ICFTU Executive Board, now have 13 out of 27.

The ICFTU, unlike its Communist competitor, is supported entirely by contributions from the members of its

[4] John P. Windmuller, "ICFTU after Ten Years: Problems and Prospects," *Industrial and Labor Relations Review*, January 1961. I have drawn from this excellent article in this and the following chapter.

affiliated unions. It accepts no government funds. Income from affiliation fees totals about $500,000 a year. Roughly $3 million a year in addition is raised for the Confederation's International Solidarity Fund. This fund is used for direct assistance to non-Communist trade unions. Most of it is spent in the developing world.

With strong urging by American labor, the ICFTU decentralized its operations and expanded its regional activity. It maintains regional organizations in Europe, the Western Hemisphere, and Asia, and in 1960 established one in Africa. In addition, it has set up local offices in key cities of Africa and Asia. It runs two full-time colleges to train trade-union leaders in Calcutta, India, and Kampala, Uganda, and conducts a number of training courses and seminars all over the world, reaching probably several thousand trade unionists a year. It has held congresses and conferences in the less-developed world to offer help in the solution of workers' problems and has sent many missions abroad for this purpose. The ICFTU is especially active in representing the interests of free labor in the United Nations and its specialized agencies, particularly the International Labor Organization. In addition, it is active in regional economic and social meetings of various sorts.

The meager resources available to the ICFTU, however, mean that its total contribution is marginal. How much, after all, can be done around the world with a few million dollars a year? In two years of operation, for example, the trade-union college in Calcutta organized only three twelve-week courses for a total of eighty-six students, although in addition it did provide some short field training programs for about eight hundred students in India, Ceylon, Indonesia, Japan, and Pakistan. Despite recent activity in the educational and training field, the ICFTU's Asian organization is still frail, largely because of a lack of leadership and enthusiasm among many of its Asian affiliates. Likewise, although there has been a marked improvement recently, its Latin American regional organization, ORIT (Organización Regional Interamericana de Trabajadores), has had a difficult time for several reasons: (1) the desire of some Latin American trade unions to remain uncommitted internationally; (2) ORIT's unfortunate past entanglements with some corrupt elements in the hierarchy of labor and government; (3) anti-Americanism and the reluctance of some Latin American organizations to become associated with U.S. trade unions for fear of becoming dominated by them; and (4) ORIT's lack of the funds and resources to provide the assistance that was hoped for, because Latin American views were frequently in conflict with those of the Brussels ICFTU headquarters. The ICFTU's African operation has long been complicated by serious division of opinion between British and American trade-union leaders concerning Africa and now is confronted by the rising challenge of "neutralism." At a 1960 meeting of the Executive Committee in Lagos, however, the African Regional Organization (AFRO) resolved to greatly intensify and coordinate assistance to ICFTU-affiliated organizations in Africa, encourage other trade-union centers to join the world free trade-union movement, and cooperate with the International Trade Secretariats in building up unions in particular industries. Solidarity Fund expenditures have perhaps been most effective, contributing to organizing drives in a number of countries. They have been used, for example, to help the cause of Algerian workers, consistent with the ICFTU's policy against all kinds of colonialism.

ICFTU policy is quite clear on oppression or dictatorship of any sort and it is outspoken in defense of freedom. At its Lagos meeting the Executive Committee of AFRO adopted a resolution condemning attempts by subversive forces to interfere in the internal affairs of national trade-union organizations, or to assimilate free trade unions, under "the pretext of Pan-Africanism," into "a type of organization which would only serve the political aims of certain governments." In early 1961, Omer Becu made a personal appeal in the name of the ICFTU to the Spanish Minister of Justice on behalf of seventy-two trade unionists on trial in Barcelona for what Becu referred to as "activities connected with the reorganization of trade-union bodies which would clearly be considered perfectly legitimate in any democratic country." In a statement issued after the seizure of the Portuguese ship "Santa Maria" by opponents of Portuguese Premier António de Oliveira Salazar, the ICFTU maintained that the incident had "thrown into vivid relief the anomaly of the continued existence in Europe of another regime as thoroughly reactionary as that of Franco, and similarly supported by a number of democratic governments of the free world."

In Latin America, ORIT incessantly condemns the efforts of "reactionaries" and "Communist totalitarianism" against inter-American democracy, and regularly offers material and moral support to those seeking freedom for Cuba, the Dominican Republic, Paraguay, and Haiti. It strongly opposed Perón in Argentina, Odría in Peru, Pérez Jiménez in Venezuela, Rojas Pinilla in Colombia and Somoza in Nicaragua. Former ORIT General Secretary Alfonso Sánchez Madariaga denounced the execution of trade-union leaders by Castro, declaring that the very men he had shot had fought with Castro against Batista and that their only "plot" had been "to maintain trade union freedom and prevent their organization from falling into the hands of agents of Moscow." [5]

The ICFTU, however, can only be as strong as its affiliates, and its affiliates are so dispersed and represent so many different economic and political commitments and motivations

[5] *Inter-American Labor Bulletin,* March 1961.

that division and dissension are constantly gnawing at its foundations. Non-Communist unions, however independent, reflect their national interest, some more than others, and this fact too accounts for considerable strain within the Confederation. Before examining the record of the AFL-CIO in these and other matters, we need to sketch the activities of another set of free labor's international instruments.

The International Trade Secretariats

The International Trade Secretariats are federations of national trade unions operating in the same or related trades or industries. Many ITS [6] were formed in the last century. Over the years they have developed a high degree of cohesion and solidarity among their members. They are giving increasing organizational assistance to expand and strengthen their constituent unions. Lately some of the Secretariats have initiated housing and cooperative programs for this purpose. Because of the industrial or occupational affinity of their affiliates, the Secretariats can concentrate primarily on the practical problems relating to their particular calling, minimizing political disagreements and friction. They cooperate with the ICFTU and have established a liaison office of their own, with a permanent secretary and headquarters in Geneva. While generally the ITS are as strongly anti-Communist as the ICFTU, they have steadfastly maintained their independence from it and have avoided many of its political entanglements. As a result, there are ITS members in areas where the ICFTU has been unable or unwilling to move, such as Burma, the U.A.R., South Africa, and Yugoslavia. Flexibility, inner cohesion, and conviction make the Secretariats especially effective anti-Communist organizations in the so-called neutralist

[6] The abbreviation is used for both singular and plural.

areas and thus extremely important to United States objectives.

Nearly forty American unions belong to seventeen ITS and are active in their work and leadership. Among the most significant of these is the International Federation of Plantation, Agricultural and Allied Workers, formed in 1959 by the merger of two former agricultural Secretariats. The jurisdiction of this federation extends not only to farm and plantation workers but also to factory workers in closely related industries, such as jute and sisal. The IFPAAW thus is in contact with the illiterate and poverty-stricken peasant masses which form the great majority of workers in developing countries, and which are prime targets of communism, especially in Latin America. The task of IFPAAW is made unusually difficult by the lack of experience in organizing plantation workers in Europe and North America. WFTU organizers, on the other hand, have had perhaps most experience in this area.

The plantation workers' Secretariat now has 41 affiliates in 36 countries and a membership of close to 4 million. The members of these unions pay regular dues, have a strong sense of participation in and loyalty to their union, meet employers face to face and bargain collectively, and are forming the basis of permanent social institutions in their communities, committed to social justice and freedom. The brightest star of IFPAAW is its extraordinary general secretary, Tom Bavin, formerly with the British Landworkers' Union, who has contributed as much to the cause of freedom as any trade-union leader. In a short time he has had remarkable success organizing strong unions of impoverished peasants in Asia and Africa. More recently he has directed his attention to Latin America. Bavin has said to me:

> We can organize the impoverished. If we don't, you can be sure the Communists will. In two years we have built a strong union of plantation workers in Tanganyika, for example. The

peasants used to be treated like children by the employers. Now they sit down with them with a new spirit of self-respect and confidence to bargain out their differences. In two years we got a 50 per cent increase in wages and incidentally a comparable increase in production. It's a question of getting hold of the right people and backing them to the hilt. We've had great success too on the tea and coffee plantations in Kenya and in Uganda and Nyasaland. Right now I'm trying to get my boys cheap houses—cement mixed with earth—which they can put up in a week. This would be a tremendous thing.

Perhaps Bavin's most famous exploit took place after World War II when he went to Malaya and organized what has become the most powerful democratic worker organization in South Asia, the Malayan Rubber Workers' Union. "I picked three men to start with," he said, "and worked shoulder to shoulder with them in the jungle. They did the job. They were the right men, of course." Bavin was helped in Malaya and in Singapore too by George L-P Weaver, currently U.S. Assistant Secretary of Labor for International Affairs, then an official of the CIO. As we have seen, the rubber workers played a central role in preventing Malaya's overthrow by the Communists. With help, IFPAAW's opportunities in the future are almost limitless.

Another important ITS, the Miners' International Federation, has 32 affiliates in 28 countries representing some 2.5 million coal and ore miners. (The American affiliate is the United Mine Workers.) It has a permanent staff of seven and its annual budget is only $70,000, but it can count on additional assistance from its affiliates when the need arises.

Eighty per cent of MIF membership growth since World War II has come from the less-developed countries. That is where MIF concentrates most of its efforts, assisting miners' unions in their struggle for higher wages and better and safer working conditions and training promising young men for international labor work. The MIF has been especially active in Ghana and Northern Rhodesia and maintains permanent offices in Nigeria and India. In the Western Hemisphere it assists the Inter-American Mine Workers' Federation.

One of the most active of all the Secretariats, the International Federation of Petroleum Workers was organized in 1954 largely through the initiative of O. A. Knight and Loyd Haskins of the Oil, Chemical and Atomic Workers, AFL-CIO. With headquarters in Denver, it has 31 affiliates in 24 countries, including both the U.A.R. and Israel; an Egyptian, Anwar Salama, is one of its eleven vice presidents. It maintains permanent offices in Bogotá, Singapore, and Karachi, with two more about to open in Africa. Largely staffed by Americans, it assists its affiliates in collective bargaining and during strike situations.

The International Metalworkers' Federation, founded in 1893, has 25 affiliates in 24 countries and a membership of more than 8 million, nearly half of which is in the United States. It still has a very small membership beyond the frontiers of Europe and North America, although it has provided valuable assistance in organizing metal workers in Nigeria. The IMF has a peculiarly important opportunity to organize strong, non-Communist trade unions in the new steel plants of India, and has recently embarked on an effective, well-financed campaign in Latin America with full-time representatives in Mexico City and other cities.

The Postal, Telegraph and Telephone International was started in 1911 and has a membership of almost 2 million in 96 unions in 55 countries. It has worked extremely effectively in Latin America and has encouraged unions in Ecuador to press for a self-help worker housing program, of which we shall say more later.

The Public Services International is especially important in Africa where, as we have seen, government workers form such an important labor group. Its work in Kenya and Nigeria has been especially important. Arnold Zander, president of the American PSI affiliate, the American Federation of State, County and Municipal Employes, has taken an active part in the work of the Secretariat and expects the ITS to increase its activity in Kenya, Zanzibar, Pemba, Nyasaland, and Madagascar in East Africa, and Sierra Leone and Gambia in the West. The PSI has also done effective work in Latin America, especially Panama where it maintains a full-time official. The influence of such an ITS among intelligent, literate, and vocal government workers in these areas is quite obviously of the utmost political as well as economic significance.

The International Transport Workers' Federation, organized in 1896, has been over the years one of the most effective of all the Trade Secretariats. It has permanent offices throughout Asia, Africa, and Latin America, and has 230 affiliates in 70 countries with a membership of 7 million. It has 30 full-time employees. In 1954 and 1955 it gave vital support to the strikes of the Karachi dockers, Japanese textile workers, Icelandic trawlermen, and the Curaçao mine workers. In 1957 it helped bring about the release of Israeli seamen and fishermen being held by Egyptian authorities for trespassing; and Ecuadorian railway workers were helped in their fight with the government to establish a free trade union.

We have already mentioned the work of the ITF vigilante committees during the Marshall Plan days. Another example of similar international strength was its successful efforts to ensure that sailors on board vessels flying so-called "flags of convenience" to escape high labor costs are protected by collective bargaining agreements. The ITF is ready and able to enforce this policy by staging a worldwide ocean transport boycott if necessary. In the ITF, as in other Secretariats, American unions have made an important contribution, in this case the railway workers and especially Arthur E. Lyon, their international representative.

The American Federation of Labor—1940-1956

Since the early days of World War II, American labor has been active in international affairs, seeking to help free trade-union movements around the world. In 1940 the AFL established the Labor League for Human Rights for "war relief purposes" and "the support of labor causes everywhere." In 1944, it established the Free Trade Union Committee as an organization within the League "to take an aggressive and direct part in reviving the free trade union movement." Its members were George Meany, William Green, David Dubinsky, and Matthew Woll. Jay Lovestone became the committee's executive secretary and guiding spirit. Lovestone, who in the 1920s was national secretary of the American Communist party, was expelled from the party in 1929 because of his refusal to accept dictation from Moscow and later became a zealous anti-Communist. His firsthand experience with the Communist movement and widespread knowledge of labor abroad made him an extremely effective anti-Communist leader and a trusted and resourceful adviser to the AFL on international matters. Another key appointment to the staff of the FTUC was that of Irving Brown, an old associate of Lovestone's who played a key role in the development of European trade unions after the war. Subsequently he was active for the AFL-CIO in Africa and in 1962 was appointed to represent the ICFTU at the United Nations.

In 1943 the AFL collaborated with the Congress of Industrial Organizations and the Railroad Brotherhoods in establishing the American Labor Conference on International Affairs to "study problems of the conduct of the war and the future peace from the point of view of organized labor." This, incidentally, was the first labor group in which the AFL and CIO participated jointly.

After the war, the American trade-union movement came to a basic disagreement on international labor policy. The AFL and the CIO went their separate ways and even the merger of the two organizations in 1955 has not entirely healed the breach. The CIO, as we have seen, collaborated with the major non-Communist trade unions of the world, as well as with Communist unions from the Soviet Union, in the formation of the WFTU. The AFL refused to join the WFTU because it believed it impossible for free trade unions to work successfully with Communists, and also because it resented the CIO's claim to speak for U.S. labor. In 1949, when the CIO and all other free trade unions rejected the WFTU as a Communist-dominated front organization, it appeared that the AFL had been right.

In the meantime, the AFL initiated a program, first in Europe and then in Latin America, to halt the spread of communism. Its foreign activities had four main features.[7] First, the AFL began an unrelenting attack on the WFTU. It fought it in the United Nations and in Germany. Perhaps most important, it took full advantage of the split within the WFTU, created by Communist animosity to the Marshall Plan, to hasten the organization's breakup, and then led in the formation of the ICFTU. Second, the AFL urged its affiliates to participate actively in the International Trade Secretariats in order to prevent them from coming under WFTU influence. In particular, the railway and machinist unions were active in reviving their International Secretariats and in preserving their independence. Third, the AFL channeled direct assistance to non-Communist forces in Europe and elsewhere. Finally, it helped organize a regional federation of trade unions in Latin America known as CIT to combat Lombardo Toledano's Communist-dominated CTAL. CIT was the forerunner of ORIT.

[7] Windmuller, *American Labor and the International Labor Movement, 1940 to 1953,* cited, pp. 77-79.

Beneath these activities lay the guiding principle inherited from Samuel Gompers, founder of the AFL, that a trade union should be wholly independent, free of the government, of political parties, of employers, and of the church. It did not go so far as to deny all assistance to any union that had affiliations, for example, with a political party or with a church, but made it quite clear that total independence was, in the eyes of the AFL, the right principle. An important corollary to this principle was that while the AFL would aid workers in their attempt to organize themselves, it would not dictate to them the type of organization which they should undertake. In supporting the establishment of trade unions in Japan after the war, for example, the AFL, at its 1948 convention, said that it "firmly believes that the development of responsible policies and procedures in labor, management, and community relationships is an evolutionary process, coming to fruition only after the problems of that relationship have been dealt with by the parties themselves in the light of national tradition and political, social and economic conditions." This principle, while not always observed, put the AFL on record as favoring assistance to free and independent worker organizations, taking fully into account the customs, institutions, and problems of the particular country in which the organization was located.

The assistance rendered by the AFL to its brothers around the globe was varied and substantial. Food and clothing were sent throughout the world under the AFL's Food for Freedom program, administered through CARE. Parcels were sent, for example, to refugees from East Germany following the revolt of June 17, 1953, and aid went to the victims of the Po Valley floods in Italy in 1952. During and immediately following World War II, food packages went to needy trade-union leaders throughout Europe and other material aid, including typewriters, mimeograph machines, food packages, and literature, was sent to strengthen free trade unions.

AFL offices and advisers in foreign countries played a vital role in reviving and strengthening free trade unions. Irving Brown and Henry Rutz in Europe, Harry Goldberg in Indonesia, Henry Kirsch in Turkey, Richard Deverall in India, the Middle East, and Japan, and Serafino Romualdi in Latin America are a few of the men who did so much for the cause of freedom in the years following World War II. Also, during the early postwar years organized labor provided specialists for a variety of governmental purposes. For example, Joseph Keenan, now secretary-treasurer of the International Brotherhood of Electrical Workers, was a special adviser to General Clay in occupied Germany and James Killen, a top official of the International Brotherhood of Pulp, Sulphite and Paper Mill Workers, served as labor adviser to General MacArthur in Japan.

Many publications, some of them translated into several languages, were sent around the world by the AFL. Some of the titles which come to mind are the *International Free Trade Union News, North American Labor News* (in Spanish), *Rodo Pacífico, Slave Labor in Russia,* and *Terror in Venezuela* (Pérez Jiménez). Assistance was provided to train foreign labor leaders and bring trade unionists from all over the world to the United States. In addition, the AFL with the CIO helped support many private organizations dedicated to keeping alive resistance groups, helping trade unionists exiled by dictators, and assisting democratic leaders in a variety of ways.

The AFL carried its fight against totalitarianism into the UN and the ILO with vigor and effectiveness, protesting any violation of trade-union rights whether it was in the Soviet Union or in the Panama Canal Zone. It protested with equal force the seizure of unions in Czechoslovakia by the Communists in 1948 and the suppression of free trade unions in Peru, Venezuela, Argentina, and Cuba.

The Congress of Industrial Organizations—1940-1956

During this same period, the CIO was also active abroad. But there were important differences between its foreign operations and those of the AFL. The CIO relied more heavily on international bodies such as the WFTU until 1949, and then the ICFTU, for implementing its foreign programs. It never maintained as great a number of permanent representatives abroad as the AFL. It showed a more sympathetic attitude than the AFL toward unions which were affiliated with political parties, and enjoyed great rapport with some of the foreign Socialist labor groups. Contributing to this was the industrial structure of the CIO and the quite unsubstantiated belief that the CIO was more in line with Socialist ideology.

In 1954 alone the CIO spent more than $500,000 to send equipment to unionists in such countries as the Philippines, the Gold Coast, Singapore, Tunisia, Morocco, and Pakistan, including typewriters, mimeograph machines, and even a printing press. CARE food packages were sent to trade unions in thirty countries. The CIO Community Service Committee sent money for relief activities during the disastrous Dutch and Honduran floods. The CIO also had an active publication and education program, sending the *CIO News* abroad in four languages and supporting a workers' exchange program. But much of this work was channeled through the ICFTU.

Walter Reuther, President of the CIO, his brother Victor, Elmer Cope, Michael Ross, James Carey, Jacob Potofsky, and Joseph Beirne were among the CIO leaders who visited foreign countries in an effort to strengthen free trade unions in their fight against communism. Cope and Victor

Reuther were stationed in Europe as CIO representatives for several years. As we have already mentioned, George Weaver traveled to Singapore and Malaya in 1955 to give vital assistance to the ICFTU unions in those areas. Like the AFL, the CIO strongly encouraged its unions to take an active part in the work of the International Trade Secretariats, and many of them played a critical role in the revival of these organizations.

The AFL-CIO from 1956 to the Present

The merger of the AFL and the CIO in late 1955 brought the termination of the AFL's Free Trade Union Committee and its far-flung operations. The AFL agreed to direct more, if not most, of its international efforts through the ICFTU, its regional organizations, and the Trade Secretariats. The International Affairs Department of the AFL-CIO was assigned the functions of the FTUC, and many of the unilateral activities of the AFL and the CIO were taken over by AFL-CIO member unions acting through Trade Secretariats. This decision has made the ITS organizations the most powerful force in international labor activity today.

During 1960 and 1961 the AFL-CIO spent about a million and a half dollars for international activities, roughly 8 per cent of the federation's income. This money, it should be remembered, is made up of the dimes and dollars of American union members and represents their commitment to their fellow workers around the world. This fact gives these funds a very special meaning to the recipients and partially accounts for the fact that no segment of our society is as respected and admired in the developing areas of the world as the American labor movement. Many of our trade unions and their leaders hold a very special place in the hearts of millions of poverty-stricken and illiterate people around the world. They represent a fine example of individual private sacrifice in the pursuit of our national objectives and cherished principles.

Most, but by no means all, of the international appropriation of the AFL-CIO is expended through the ICFTU or its regional organizations, especially ORIT. Africa and Asia have also received substantial direct aid from the AFL-CIO, which has been the cause of some serious resentment on the part of the British Trades Union Congress (see pp. 99-100). In 1957 the AFL-CIO gave important help to Tom Mboya, for example, and $50,000 was allocated to help train East African trade-union leaders, some of whom came to the United States for one year of combined academic study and trade-union training. A similar program was launched for Latin America. These programs were terminated as the result of ICFTU pressure on American labor to reduce its unilateral activity, but they led to the establishment of the ICFTU college at Kampala.

In 1960 the AFL-CIO gave $180,000 for the establishment of the Afro-Asian Institute for Labor Studies in Israel, one of the most effective centers for helping trade unionists from less-developed countries in the world today (see pp. 41-42). In addition, the AFL-CIO and its member unions have contributed, via CARE, hospital supplies, jeeps, mimeograph machines, typewriters, training aids, films, books, and material of all sorts to unions throughout the developing world. Most recently these supplies have gone to Kenya, Algeria, Morocco, Cameroon, Nigeria, Malaya, Guinea, the Congo, Hong Kong, and Korea. The AFL-CIO and individual unions gave more than $50,000 to help resettle Hungarian refugees. It also aided Cuban refugees and victims of the Chilean earthquake in 1960. It has sent its leaders throughout the world. American labor officials have manned the labor exhibits at United States trade fairs in Asia, Africa, and Latin America. Many of them are in the foreign service as labor attachés in our embassies.

As before the merger, the AFL-CIO continues to be active in the United Nations and the ILO, pressing the cause of freedom and trade-union rights at every juncture. American labor played a leading part in securing a UN-ILO study on forced labor in the Soviet Union, in ousting the Hungarian delegation from the ILO conference two years in a row, and in condemning violations of freedom of association wherever they might occur.

Individual U.S. unions have also done important work abroad. The railway unions have been active primarily through the International Transport Workers' Federation. The Letter Carriers and the Communications Workers, with other U.S. affiliates of the Postal, Telegraph and Telephone Trade Secretariat, conducted a school for South American trade unionists in Front Royal, Virginia, to train them in leadership so that they in turn can train their fellows at home to build strong, stable, independent unions. An additional $10,000 has been pledged by the PTTI for Asian work. The Amalgamated Clothing Workers of America has given substantial assistance to the Israeli labor federation, and also to trade unions in Italy. The union helped its Italian brothers build a cooperative clothing factory at the cost of $250,000, a Boys' Town near Palermo, and it set up a Hands-across-the-Sea Italian refugee program to help Italian tailors and their families migrate to America where their skills were needed. In Asia, Latin America, and Europe the International Ladies' Garment Workers' Union has spent well over $1 million in the last three years to provide assistance to non-Communist trade unions. The executive board of the United Automobile Workers voted to spend $1.5 million of the interest on the union's strike fund to help in the organization of workers abroad, especially through the International Metalworkers' Federation. There are many more examples of American unions active abroad, including those of the electrical workers (IUE and IBEW), steelworkers, machinists, maritime workers, mine workers, oil, chemical and atomic workers, retail clerks, and state, county and municipal workers, to name but a few. In Latin America especially, the food and drink unions, the musicians, the stagehands and entertainment workers, and the newspaper guild have made considerable efforts recently. The influence of the AFL-CIO directly on United States foreign policy is plainly great. It has pressed consistently for a stronger attitude by the government against colonialism; advocated a free Algeria; urged a boycott of South Africa; insisted on a firm policy against dictators of the right or left; supported a strong anti-Communist line, a free Berlin, a liberal trade policy, and has been outstanding in its support of increased foreign aid. It has been opposed to the recognition of Red China. It saw Castro for what he was long before it became apparent to many. At every crucial turn, regardless of the party in power, American labor has been a firm voice for national unity.

In addition, indirectly, through its own operations and contributions around the world, the AFL-CIO has exemplified an America which is interested in the worker, his trade union, and his right to organize in order to secure a better life for himself and his family. It has provided funds at the grass roots to those organizations that will determine the future of many countries in the world today. It has sent its people abroad, sometimes for long periods of time to work shoulder to shoulder with the trade unionists in the developing world in their struggle for freedom, independence, and social justice. It has, in short, rendered a great service. But has this been enough? Could there be improvement? What more should be done in the future? These questions must be faced squarely and frankly.

* * *

The lines of battle are drawn.

On one side is a single effort, backed by the great resources of a bloc of nations, centrally directed, ably led, unbothered by principles of any sort, willing to adopt any guise, change any policy, go to any lengths to subvert and overthrow every non-Communist system. Furthermore, communism offers a utopian solution to the poverty and injustice plaguing the developing countries, and an apparently impressive example in the Soviet Union which between 1950 and 1960 reportedly doubled its total production, increased its agricultural production 50 per cent and its standards of living by about two-thirds.[8]

On the other side is a collection of organizations, largely uncoordinated, certainly not centrally directed, each with separate interests, loyal to separate systems and states, unified by a general commitment to freedom, independence, and social justice, but divided as to the best methods of fulfilling this commitment.

[8] *The New York Times,* May 11, 1961, editorial reporting on the Princeton Conference on the Soviet economy.

Chapter IV

UNITY VS. DIVERSITY—
FREE LABOR'S PROBLEMS

Communist efforts in the international labor field benefit from the well-known advantages of dictatorial discipline. WFTU meetings are smooth and well directed. Anybody can come and generally get his way paid. Controversy is kept out of the way, smothered by long speeches on the evils of colonialism, imperialism, money-grubbing capitalists, and the West in general. Funds flow freely to those who will do the Communists' bidding. Frequently what the Communists ask is not too difficult: "Preserve your country and its labor movement from outside interference; don't affiliate with any outside group—us or anyone else; conduct your unions as you like. If you want to tie yourself to a political party, do so; if you want to bargain collectively, do so; if you want to build hospitals and houses, fine. We will help you. In return all we ask is that our local agents be given a place in your operation so that we can help you better. They speak your language and understand your problems."

To plantation workers, the Communists say: "We have had agricultural experience like that of no other nation in the world. We have come from being a starving people to a nation of plenty in a short time. We are willing and able to work with you in the fields and help you organize your unions."

To the industrial workers, they say: "We in the Soviet Union have doubled our production and raised our standard of living dramatically in the past ten years. Of course, along the way we suffered privation but it was no worse than yours today."

Labor from the democracies, on the other hand, presents quite a different picture and offers quite a different package. It enjoys the advantages but suffers the handicap of free peoples in that it is pluralistic and without central discipline. The highly developed trade unions of Western Europe and the United States are making a variety of individual efforts in Africa, Asia, and Latin America. In many cases they are trying to sell a particular brand of trade unionism. Important elements of U.S. labor, still guided by the principles set forth by Samuel Gompers, and unaware of or unconcerned with labor's experience when the United States was an underdeveloped country, sometimes seek to persuade trade unions to sever their ties with governments and political parties, whether or not the unions have the strength, organization, and leadership required to do so. Many times U.S. labor offers its own example as the best and the right one for the less-developed world to follow. British and German unions, of course, offer a different example.

Then there is the ICFTU, whose meetings, unlike those of the WFTU, are feasts of controversy and dispute. This is not unusual for democratic gatherings and there would be something wrong if it were otherwise, but the nature of the controversy bears analysis. Given the large role played by the major trade unions of Western Europe and the United States, the ICFTU is seriously torn by many of the same basic differences which trouble the NATO countries. Trade unions from whatever country represent many of the attitudes and policies of their governments even though they may be entirely independent of them. In addition, they have differing attitudes of their own. In the United States there is by no means complete agreement on international labor policies, even within the AFL-CIO itself.

Division in American Labor

While the merger of the AFL and CIO is undoubtedly an accomplished fact, there is still strong and bitter rivalry between the two factions. It is particularly strong in international affairs. There have even been instances in ICFTU meetings where the AFL and CIO factions of the theoretically single American delegation voted in different ways on the same issue.

While both factions are unalterably opposed to communism, they have substantially different views about how to cope with it. The CIO faction feels that the AFL line is too negative, bombastic, and moralizing. It feels that AFL leaders tend to see Red agents where there are none and are so obsessed with communism that they neglect to put sufficient emphasis on the positive work that must be done around the world to strengthen the cause of freedom. Whereas the CIO regards itself as taking a more sophisticated, constructive attitude toward world problems, the AFL group tends to look upon some CIO leaders as dupes, unaware of the hard realities of the cold war. One cannot avoid wondering whether, however unfairly, the CIO's willingness to join Soviet trade unions in the WFTU in 1945 does not still rankle in the hearts of some of the old AFL leaders and advisers. It should be remembered that many of the leading personalities of those days are still key officials on both sides of the AFL-CIO today. It should also be recalled, however, that some years before the merger the CIO rid itself of Communist party members and sympathizers.

George Meany, former president of the old AFL, was speaking partly about some of his CIO friends in 1955 when, just having been elected president of the new AFL-CIO, he made a blunt attack on "liberals" for lacking vigor in fighting Communists. He warned them against developing "a certain type of McCarthyism of their own." He went on to say: "They must shun like a plague the role of being anti-anti-Communist. . . . Only by refusing to be thus entrapped can liberals shed every vestige of subconscious and conscious regard for Communism as a movement with which they have something in common."[1]

In this same speech, made to heads of free trade unions from all over the world at a luncheon of the National Religion and Labor Foundation in New York, Mr. Meany said that no country could be neutral in the struggle between communism and democracy. "Nehru and Tito are not neutral," he said. "They are aides and allies of Communism in fact and in effect, if not in diplomatic verbiage."[2]

Walter Reuther, following Mr. Meany at the same luncheon, said that the United States must earn the right to lead the free world by showing that it was ready to end "its own ugly and immoral practices in race relations. . . . We have no right to preach morality to the world or point an accusing finger at other nations unless we are fighting equally hard against injustices at home. We must be as courageous in fighting what goes on in Mississippi as in fighting tyranny behind the Iron Curtain." Obviously Mr. Reuther, who fought hard and successfully to rid the United Automobile Workers of Communist influence in 1946, resents any suggestion that he or his colleagues are "soft" on communism. Shortly after this speech, in April of 1956, he left for India where he was garlanded and warmly welcomed by Mr. Nehru.

[1] Article by A. H. Raskin in *The New York Times*, December 14, 1955.
[2] Mr. Meany's attitude toward Prime Minister Nehru is somewhat more friendly today.

When Messrs. Mikoyan and Khrushchev made their good will tours through the United States, Mr. Meany and most of his former AFL colleagues refused to meet with them. It would have been, they felt, like lunching with gangsters. Furthermore, since there were no free trade unions in the Soviet Union, any recognition of U.S.S.R. leaders by American labor would be misunderstood by free labor abroad. Also it was their feeling that no hospitality of any sort should be shown to those who had slaughtered Hungarian workers and oppressed millions.

The Executive Council of the AFL-CIO eloquently set forth the official policy in a statement dated August 20, 1959:

> President Eisenhower has invited Nikita Khrushchev, the head of the Soviet Union, to visit the United States in the near future.
>
> From various sources there have come to us queries as to what is our attitude to the forthcoming visit of Mr. Khrushchev.
>
> It is not for the A.F.L.-C.I.O. Executive Council to approve or disapprove an invitation extended by our President to the head of another government. We do not, therefore, have any comment to make on the wisdom of the President's invitation. At the same time, we must all face the situation realistically.
>
> The Soviet regime continues to be a totalitarian dictatorship. It is dedicated to aggression and world domination. It has destroyed all democratic rights and liberties in its own country. It is now seeking to subvert and destroy the rights and liberties which we Americans cherish dearly in our country.
>
> There is not a shred of evidence to show that the Kremlin rulers have changed the nature or aims of their regime or even slackened their drive to conquer the world and remold it on the pattern of Soviet tyranny.
>
> It has been reported that Vice President Nixon, during his visit to the U.S.S.R., indicated he would urge American labor to join actively in an exchange program with the so-called un-

ions of Soviet Russia. It is, therefore, necessary to set the record straight.

In this situation, the Executive Council reaffirms its declaration of February, 1959, against exchanging delegations with dictatorship countries. We further reiterate our whole-hearted support of the I.C.F.T.U. (International Confederation of Free Trade Unions) policy against exchanges of delegations with the so-called trade unions in Communist or any other totalitarian countries.

The A.F.L.-C.I.O. is an organization of free trade unions. There are no Soviet counterparts with which we of the A.F.L.-C.I.O. can have such exchanges. The Kremlin dictatorship strictly prohibits the Soviet workers from organizing free trade unions. The so-called trade unions in the U.S.S.R. are nothing but agencies of the Communist dictatorship.

Consequently, it is out of the question for the A.F.L.-C.I.O. to give recognition to the head of a government which does not permit its own workers to have any free trade unions. American labor could never participate in honoring the head of a government which seeks to destroy human freedom in any form.

Furthermore, as a free trade union movement, the A.F.L.-C.I.O. is not bound to agree with every domestic or foreign policy of our Government.

For example, the American labor movement has always firmly opposed U.S. recognition of the Franco dictatorship. But our Government has recognized and has even given economic aid to this dictatorship. Such governmental actions do not mean that the A.F.L.-C.I.O. should welcome Franco to our shores in the event our Government should ever invite him to visit the United States.

By the same token the President's invitation to Mr. Khrushchev does not mean that the A.F.L.-C.I.O. should participate in honoring this head of a foreign government which runs a vast network of forced labor camps and which ordered the murder of thousands of Hungarians fighting for their national independence and freedom.[3]

[3] Text of resolution reprinted in *The New York Times,* August 21, 1959.

While this was the policy of the AFL-CIO, in reality it was nearer the policy of the AFL than the CIO. No less anti-Communist, CIO leaders felt it was important to confront the Soviet leaders with their infamous activities, argue with them, and show them up before the world. Mr. Reuther and his colleagues gave Chairman Khrushchev the most difficult hours of his visit, just as they had Mr. Mikoyan before him. The following excerpts of the conversation provide some insights into the CIO position:

KHRUSHCHEV: . . . The United States exploits the wealth of other countries, under-developed countries, for profits. England and France do the same. They exploit the wealth of countries that need aid. We do not exploit any country—we only engage in trade.

REUTHER: You exploit the workers of East Germany.

KHRUSHCHEV: Where did you dream that up?

REUTHER: If you don't exploit them, why should 3,000,000 of them cross the border into West Germany?

KHRUSHCHEV: You are hopelessly sick with capitalist fever.

* * *

REUTHER: The workers in West Germany are free.

KHRUSHCHEV: We are free, too.

REUTHER: Do you have credentials to speak for the workers of the world?

KHRUSHCHEV: Do you have credentials to poke your nose into East Germany?

CAREY [President of the International Union of Electrical, Radio and Machine Workers]: This is part of our difficulty: the fear of the Chairman that the United States actually wants to dominate the world.

KHRUSHCHEV: Not just wants—striving!

CAREY: And the other way around, there is the fear in the United States, based on much evidence, that the Soviet Union wants to dominate the world.

KHRUSHCHEV: The Soviet ruble does not kow-tow to the American dollar. [At this point, Khrushchev raised his voice loudly and vehemently.] You have been spoiled by everyone bowing down, by everyone cringing and crawling.

❊   ❊   ❊

REUTHER: I worked with the anti-Hitler underground in Germany before going to Russia. What bothers me about your social system is not that you're not making economic progress for the workers and peasants. You're making tremendous technical progress. And I know all about your rationale of workers not striking against themselves. But the Chairman himself exposed—in his exposure of Stalin's crimes—the cult and power of an individual. How could the worker in that period get justice if he would not strike or publicly protest?

KHRUSHCHEV: His trade union.

REUTHER: The union is an extension of government, the Soviet Government. Does a union ever disagree with the Government? Can you give us one single example in which one of your unions ever disagreed with Government policy?

KHRUSHCHEV: Why poke your nose into our business?

REUTHER: Freedom is everybody's business—you are always expressing a concern for the workers of Asia. There is a thing called international labor solidarity. When I was in Russia I was a member of a union, and it was what we would call a company union.

(Fast and frequently indignant interchanges between the Chairman and the labor side of the table, too fast to be recorded.)

REUTHER: Everytime we push a sharp question, the Chairman gets angry.

KHRUSHCHEV (getting red in face, and just slightly loud): And what we call what you represent—capitalist lackeys.

❊   ❊   ❊

FELLER [President of the United Brewery Workers]: Mr. Chairman, I cannot understand since the Communist party proclaims itself to be the liberator of the working class, yet we see mass exodus of workers in other countries following the Communist seizure of power. You have the example of 3,000,000 workers fleeing from East Germany to West Berlin, and about 3,000,000 fleeing from North Korea to South Korea, and as mentioned a moment ago, 300 or so thousands of Hungarians braved arrest and death in escaping to freedom. Mr. Khrushchev, can you tell us of a single instance where, following Communist seizure of power, there has been a mass influx of workers from surrounding non-Communist countries into the Communist country? If the Communist party is the liberator of the working class, why don't we see this phenomenon?

KHRUSHCHEV: Is that all? Think it over. Drink your beer. Perhaps that will help you to find the answer to your question.[4]

It is hard to say which of the two approaches of American labor toward communism is more effective, the AFL's absolute and uncompromising refusal of contact, or the CIO's contact for argument's sake. It is certain, however, that this difference in viewpoint, representing as it does a deep division not only within the AFL-CIO but also in the ICFTU and other international organizations, is harmful. It is exploited by the Communists as are all points of division in the free world, and used as a lever to pry apart those who are basically in agreement.

Despite the differing viewpoints, however, American labor sent Mr. Khrushchev home with no reason to believe that the workers of the United States were the exploited proletariat which he had described, or were in any way prepared to have their grandchildren live under communism.

The Problem of Exchanges

As we have seen, the Communist international labor effort consists of a vigorous "peace and unity" drive by the WFTU and increasing attempts to encourage exchanges of visits between worker organizations in the free and Com-

---

[4] This account was made and edited by the AFL-CIO participants. *The New York Times*, September 22, 1959.

munist countries.[5] The ICFTU is feeling the full brunt of these two campaigns. Until now its firm position has been wholehearted resistance to both efforts. Increasingly, however, trade unions from the developing countries are arguing: Why, if the WFTU is willing to cooperate with us in certain areas in the pursuit of social justice, should we not work with them? There is also some sentiment for "summit meetings" between the two organizations to talk over common problems. American labor has taken the leadership in firmly opposing this line of argument, pointing out its disastrous consequences, but the talk continues.

A more serious aspect of Western labor disunity is the increasing desire on the part of many constituent members of the important ICFTU affiliates, including those from Belgium, Britain, India, and Israel, to exchange fraternal delegations with Communist countries. Trade unions in each of these countries sent fraternal delegations to the meeting of the Yugoslav Labor Federation in 1959, and a number of ICFTU affiliates have already established formal relationships with worker organizations in Poland and Yugoslavia. The Australian Council of Trade Unions has for some time been sending representatives to labor meetings in Moscow and Peking, declaring that the ICFTU has no business telling members of an affiliate where and whom they shall visit. American labor itself was sorely embarrassed in the summer of 1960 when Joseph Curran, a vice president of the AFL-CIO and president of the National Maritime Union of America, visited the Soviet Union and talked with Khrushchev. Other lower-ranking American labor officials have also made the trek eastward. This is especially serious because as more and more Americans violate AFL-CIO and ICFTU policy in this regard, it becomes easier for trade unionists from Asia, Africa, and Latin America to do the same and visit

[5] John P. Windmuller, "ICFTU after Ten Years: Problems and Prospects," *Industrial and Labor Relations Review,* January 1961.

the Sino-Soviet bloc with impunity. Such visits tend to blur the distinctions between real trade unions and Communist puppet organizations. Taking it one step further, when this distinction becomes unclear, confusion follows about the distinction between a free economy and one controlled by the state, between tyranny and democracy, imperialism and nationalism, dignity and degradation. It is this sort of obscurity which communism requires to camouflage its purposes and achieve its goals.

While the policy line of American labor and the ICFTU is still theoretically firm on the question of trade union visits and exchanges, the continual stream of infringements of the policy would appear to forecast a breakdown in the future unless strong action is taken.

Issues in Dispute

One of the most debilitating divisions in the ICFTU structure is that between the AFL-CIO and the British Trades Union Congress. This is an old quarrel, comparable in some respects to that between the two factions of the AFL-CIO itself.

The British, although opposed to communism, take a quite different approach to it than do the Americans. Many leaders of British labor do not feel that because a man is a Communist he is necessarily an agent of a foreign power. There are many examples in Britain today, they say, of loyal subjects of the Queen who are Communists. An official British source estimated that one out of every ten British trade union officials is a card-carrying member of the party. These men have been duly elected by their membership, which is not Communist, and, they say, are perfectly capable of opposing the forces of international communism in Africa, Asia, or anywhere else. The TUC feels that if a trade union leader in Africa, for example, is doing a good job, ably assisting a democratic worker organization, he should not be deprived of ICFTU assistance just because he happens to be associated with the Communist party. The Communist party, they argue, is just another political party. To the American labor movement this notion is quite unbelievable, unacceptable, and totally wrong. Communism is an international conspiracy. If you are a member of the party and do not conform to its discipline and instructions, you are expelled. It is quite inconceivable for a man to be a Communist and not loyal to Moscow or Peking. Communist doctrine would certainly appear to support the American view on this question.

There are other differences too. The Americans feel many British and European trade unionists have an insufficient realization of the need for an improved and expanded NATO defense system. The "better Red than dead" philosophy of Bertrand Russell, shared by some trade unionists, is completely unacceptable to Americans. They differ also on the question of Red China's recognition and admittance to the UN. And American labor, long a foe of colonialism, feels that some British and European trade unionists are overly defensive about the vanishing colonies of their native land. Europeans on their part are appalled sometimes at the aggressive anticommunism of American labor. They are cynical about the true purposes of American trade unionists in Africa and Asia, and are offended by the slurs and allegations that they have been laggard in their efforts to obtain freedom for their colonial brothers.

Apart from these ideological differences there are other sources of resentment between British and American labor, mostly centering around American activity in Africa. British trade unionists are jealous and proud of their ties with African trade unions and the assistance they rendered to them before independence. They feel a sense of responsibility for their continued growth and resent American interference in what they regard as their territory. They are particularly angered by what they charge has been the American practice of sending its agents around Africa, and India also, handing out large sums of money to individuals who are then expected to build trade unions the American way. American trade union assistance to Tom Mboya in Kenya has probably irritated the British most. The TUC regards Mboya as a good man but a politician, not a trade unionist. It favors building worker organizations from the bottom up, helping them to achieve strength and to elect their own leaders. The Americans, they charge, try to build from the top down, picking the leaders and then helping them to construct a trade union.

The AFL-CIO, however, feels that its long-standing position against colonialism gives it a special appeal in Africa and that its assistance to African trade unionists is not only quite appropriate but useful. It feels that it is naïve to talk of building trade unions only from the bottom up. While assistance at the basic level is, of course, important, leaders who have the capacity to form an organization where none exists or re-form one that may be faltering, must also be encouraged. The Americans argue that assistance to Tom Mboya, for example, who has become a leading figure in the ICFTU, has not only strengthened that organization but the whole cause of freedom and democracy in Africa. That he is also a politician cannot be helped and, in fact, increases his total effectiveness in labor's fight.

This sort of dispute has led to increasing pressure on all national unions, especially the American, to channel more of their international work through the ICFTU. But the AFL-CIO has been reluctant to give up its own international activities, not being satisfied with ICFTU efforts to build and strengthen worker organizations in the newly developing countries. The ICFTU is not intensive enough, they say, and is not sufficiently militant in its opposition to communism. American labor feels that the ICFTU is apathetic, inefficient and deals too frequently with the wrong people. The secretariat of the ICFTU has always viewed its organizing task as only one among a good many others, such as representation at the UN and ILO, labor education and training, pursuing protection of trade-union rights around the world, and carrying on its political struggle with governments for these rights. The ICFTU's failure to live up to the perhaps unrealistic expectations of its dominant affiliates has meant that more and more resources have been placed at the disposal of the International Trade Secretariats, many of which draw heavily on the ICFTU's Solidarity Fund for their operations.

The Secretariats have a considerable advantage over the ICFTU in many newly developing areas. Accepting aid from or affiliating with an ITS does not imply the same sort of political commitment on the part of a trade union in Africa or Latin America, for example, as would relations with the ICFTU. There is no real Communist parallel to the Secretariats.[6] There is no alternative, and while the Secretariats are anti-Communist, joining an ITS does not necessarily force a union to show its hand on the sometimes touchy questions of East-West politics. Also, the Secretariats have not been plagued to the same degree by the bitter internal fights that have impeded the ICFTU. For similar reasons they have an advantage over the AFL-CIO itself. Trade unions of many neutralist countries may be reluctant to accept aid directly from U.S. unions but not if that aid comes via an ITS.

Relationships between the ICFTU and independent regional federations, such as the All-African Trade Union Federation, are growing increasingly tense. As we have seen,

[6] It may be that the eleven Communist Trade-Union Internationals will become rivals to the ITS but so far their activities have not been pitched in that direction.

these organizations, while not strictly Communist-dominated, are stimulated and encouraged by the Communists to decrease the influence of free trade unions in developing areas. In the case of Africa, the ICFTU, quite wisely, has refrained from attacking this movement. Tom Mboya, speaking for the ICFTU and apparently also reflecting the views of the AFL-CIO, has supported an all-African federation with the understanding that members of such a federation could also, if they chose, join the ICFTU and, presumably, Trade Secretariats. A firm position opposing independent federations would not only fail to get support but would tend to sustain the Communist contention that the ICFTU is a Trojan horse for Western "imperialism."

In Latin America, on the other hand, the situation is not so clear. The AFL-CIO appears, again quite understandably, to be vigorously opposing the formation of Castro- and Communist-inspired independent federations. In February 1960, in fact, ORIT announced a "systematic counter-offensive by democratic unions against the campaign to establish new federations."

Professor John Windmuller cogently asks:

> How is one to account for this striking difference in prescriptions? . . . the AFL-CIO seems to distinguish between basic political motivations at work by noting a far stronger communist influence in Latin America than in Africa. Thus, what is considered in one area to be the inevitable consequence of nationalism, anticolonialism, and an understandable form of racialism, is viewed in the other as stemming from the unholy mixture of anti-Americanism and communism, disguised in an anti-imperialist cloak.[7]

American labor's traditional anticolonialism inspires its liberality toward independent African labor movements. The AFL-CIO sees no reason why the ICFTU should go out

[7] Windmuller, *ICFTU after Ten Years,* cited, pp. 263-264.

of its way to protect or increase ties between European and British trade unions and their African colleagues. The British TUC, however, which has long been urging freedom for all British colonies, contends that its role in strengthening democratic trade unions in Africa has been extremely valuable and has produced useful relationships which should not be disrupted by theoretically independent federations.

The shoe is very much on the other foot with regard to Latin America where the main effort of American labor has been made. For many years our labor movement has been giving vital support to ORIT and to Trade Secretariat activity in Latin America. There are few Americans who have done as much to promote freedom, democracy and the best interests of our country in that area as Serafino Romualdi, Inter-American Representative of the AFL-CIO. American labor is extremely reluctant to see this work washed out by theoretically neutralist but actually Communist-inspired organizations.

The ICFTU, therefore, appears split on the issue of regional federations, with the major national trade-union federations taking the line most representative of their country's interest and their own past commitment.

Weaknesses in Organizing

Apart from these rather important differences of view and attitude among the leaders of non-Communist labor, there are other serious weaknesses in the current effort to strengthen democratic trade unions in the developing countries.

First, in its anxiety to build up its affiliation figures, the ICFTU and its regional bodies have sometimes encouraged the growth of rather flimsy organizations. It looks good on the record to have a national trade-union center in as many countries as possible, but in some cases these units are extremely weak. They fall prey to crooks, corrupt politicians, and phonies. In too many cases money is given to the wrong person. He is told to build a union, an ICFTU affiliate. He does so frequently in such a way as to serve his own particular interest. Frequently no effort is made to collect dues. This is one cause for a lack of a sense of participation by the membership. Leadership established with a check and nothing else can generally be similarly unseated, and the membership, having had little to do with the union's establishment in the first place, scarcely knows the difference. Often a hard-driving Trade Secretariat, eager to build a strong trade union from the roots up, with a sense of participation and responsibility in its membership, will find itself in competition with a corrupt and ineffective, but perhaps politically influential, ICFTU union.

In Guatemala, for example, a number of small, uneconomic trade unions have been built up with very little organization or participation among members. There is little structure, no national cohesion, and little effort at dues collection. These unions can be destroyed as quickly as they are established, and are easy prey for any rabble-rouser.

INTUC in India is a powerful political machine for the Congress party. It also has some very strong solid elements within it, such as the Ahmedabad Textile Labor Association. While it is certainly more than merely a paper organization, INTUC membership generally is not well organized. Good leaders are scarce. Corruption is too prevalent. Most of the members of INTUC don't know who their leaders are and care less. There could be a complete shift overnight with relatively little general notice or concern.

Many feel the ICFTU has forgotten what it means to get out into the field and organize workers. Handouts, fancy programs, and publications do not make unions. The two ICFTU colleges at Calcutta and Kampala, while moving in the right direction, do not begin to meet the problems of training union members and leaders. They tend to limit their efforts to English-speaking elites, to the privileged few among labor leaders, leaving vast reservoirs of energetic young men untapped, untrained, depressed, and frustrated.

It is not primarily a question of money. Although necessary, money in the wrong hands can do more harm than good. It is a question of finding the right people who will get out into the field and do the long, hard, work of organizing strong trade unions. These people, when found, must of course be adequately backed, but there is no substitute for hard work at the grass roots.

Secondly, we should learn from the Communists that the spearhead of revolution in newly developing countries is sometimes not industrial workers but landless peasants.[8] It is in the poor farmers, the sharecroppers, the field workers, still suffering the evils of feudalism and the oppression of exploitative landowners, that the fire of revolt is burning most brightly in many parts of Asia, Africa, and especially Latin America. While revolutions are generally started and led by intellectuals—lawyers, politicians, white collar groups —it is the hopeless masses to whom the message of Castro, for example, has special appeal. These are the people whose revolution must become the mission of the United States. Their reform is our salvation and there is no time to waste.

This is why the work of Tom Bavin and the federation of plantation workers is of such crucial importance to the cause of freedom. "The future," says Bavin, "lies in bringing hope to the hopeless." He is trying to build organizations of sharecroppers in the Philippines, in Asia, and in Africa, and organizations of 50,000 *campesinos* in Brazil. He tells the story of a peasant group working on a huge estate outside Rio de Janeiro. They lived in mud houses, "squatting" where they could find a place. The landowner's private police force

[8] Barbara Ward, *India and the West* (New York: Norton, 1961), p. 93.

came along one day and razed their whole community, destroying every house, declaring they had no right to build on private land. "These people," Bavin told me, "don't know what Communism is. They have known dictatorship and now they know democracy, and they know that for them nothing has changed." It is to these people that the words of Castro are coming from the North like the call of a bugle, offering hope for a change from the age-old misery of the past, offering a chance for their children, a new life with a house and food and most of all hope.

The plantation workers' Trade Secretariat is right now working desperately to organize these *campesinos* and teach them how to band together in order to deal successfully with their employers and achieve peacefully the reforms that are otherwise bound to come violently. Bavin and his men are now trying to do in Latin America what they have done so effectively in Malaya, Tanganyika, Ceylon, and many other countries. In addition, they are encouraging the new *campesino* unions to cooperate on housing projects and are hoping to get cement and UN instruction booklets to them to help them build houses cheaply and quickly.

The Postal, Telegraph and Telephone Trade Secretariat is doing similar work in Ecuador and other countries of Latin America, but the resources are small compared to the need, and the race with communism and *Fidelismo* is too close for comfort.

It is my opinion that this type of activity by free labor is the hope of the future. Efforts like these will show the people that democracy can offer a way out of their misery, that their age-old problems can be solved within a framework of freedom, and that the West is on their side in their legitimate demands for revolution and reform.

The American labor movement, as well as its allies in Britain and Europe, must drop the stereotypes of the past and set about devising effective ways to meet the needs of the workers of the newly developing countries realistically, quickly, and with due humility. Our way is one way. It may be the best for us. But American labor should never forget the almost complete difference between the problems with which it is geared to cope today and those facing the *campesino* in Brazil, the miner in India, the rubber worker in Liberia. There just is no comparison. It is absurd to pretend there is. Some of our experience and the techniques we have developed may be useful, but much is not.

Every effort should be made to prevent the political rivalries and disagreements within the ICFTU from impeding progress in the newly developing world. While there are important and legitimate differences of opinion in the free world, no bickering over administration, jurisdiction, or prerogatives should come between free labor in the industrialized countries and its brothers in the southern half of the world. The task is too big and the stakes too high.

A New Course for ICFTU and ITS

To minimize the dissension which has crippled the ICFTU for so long and to make free labor's role more effective, I would suggest the following course of action.

Basically, unless compelling considerations require otherwise, all organizing activity and all direct assistance for the strengthening of individual worker organizations in the newly developing world should be channeled through the International Trade Secretariats. Because the Secretariats are organized by specific industries and trades, their members have a common bond that other kinds of organizations lack. ITS members are tied together, not by a shaky string of political beliefs, often all too transient, but by a common body of experience, suffering, and knowledge acquired in day-to-day work. Oil workers, coal miners, peasants, and machinists the world over share much in common with each other. They are apt to understand and care about one another. They have a practical awareness of what needs to be done and they are prepared to help one another in doing it. A peasant will help a peasant before he will a steelworker. A miner will help a miner before he will a machinist. And so on. For the basically anti-Communist Secretariats, these nonpolitical bonds are a great advantage.

Political rivalries and dissension among free world countries would, of course, not be eliminated by increasing the organizing activity of the Secretariats. There would still be conflict and disagreement in their executive direction, but it would be of a more manageable sort. An ITS is generally led by a small group of dedicated individuals; most are free of the old sores which plague ICFTU relations. They do not have the difficulties of the ICFTU's large bureaucracy which must represent virtually every non-Communist interest on the globe. They are without exception unalterably committed to freedom and democracy.

Concentration on the Secretariats would mean, quite obviously, a reduction in the organizing assistance given directly to individual trade unions by American and European labor organizations and by the ICFTU. This procedure would, however, leave American and European labor, as well as the ICFTU and its regional organizations, quite free to provide direct assistance to national trade-union centers or federations of trade unions. The work of the Secretariats and of the assistance channeled through them would be directed toward individual unions in the underdeveloped countries. This would by no means weaken the ICFTU or its regional organizations. Quite to the contrary, it would strengthen them by taking away elements of discord and leaving them to conduct the equally important work upon which there can be general agreement.

The ICFTU can do much to strengthen the Secretariats. It should continue to collect its International Solidarity

Fund and distribute it to Secretariats on a priority basis to meet most pressing needs. The ICFTU might also become a general service agency for the Secretariats, which, operating far and wide in the field, close to the people, their needs, and problems, require greatly increased backstopping. It should consider stepping up its publication program and increasing the languages in which its literature is available. It could develop a series of technical handbooks on such subjects as housing, cooperatives, and health, in addition to continuing its regular informational work on collective bargaining and organization.

The ICFTU, especially its regional organizations, should seriously consider establishing a number of training centers around the world readily accessible to new young leaders. Their courses should be conducted in local languages and should include practical instruction in the specific problems being faced in the area where they are located. The two ICFTU colleges could be continued and strengthened for higher level training of those leaders who show special promise in the smaller schools. Many of these new training centers might be mobile, going from place to place to meet the urgency of the times. In all these matters the ICFTU and its regional organization should, of course, work extremely closely with the headquarters staff of the Secretariats, not for the purpose of directing them, but in order to provide the best possible service and assistance as well as the guidance and advice necessary to make free labor's effort unified and cohesive.

In addition to its work with the Secretariats, the ICFTU should continue direct activity of its own. It should increase its concern for building strong national trade-union centers or federations and should serve as a forum for these centers. It should step up its work in the UN and the specialized agencies, representing there the interests of workers and worker organizations, seeking to ensure coordination between UN technical assistance programs and those of free labor so as to make certain that free world dollars go as far as possible. It should in all ways seek to protect and extend the rights of workers and trade unions, always keeping the attention of the world focused on the importance of strong, responsible trade unions to a free, stable, and just economic system. Directly, and particularly through its regional organizations, the ICFTU should increase its efforts with individual governments to ensure and protect labor's rights, becoming a true conscience for the world, never failing to protest a backward step or encourage a forward one on the path to social justice.

ICFTU should continue with force and clarity to fight the Communists at every juncture. For this purpose a wider unity must be reached among its more powerful members. Such unity, I think, is more likely if the ICFTU's responsibilities for organizing and direct assistance were transferred to the Secretariats. To be sure there would still be disagreement, but it would be less. The ITS is smaller and is focused on a particular group of workers. Thus it can concentrate more on technical problems and be less encumbered by political differences. For example, Israel and the United Arab Republic sit together in the oil workers' ITS and progress results. With such a reorganization of its forces, free labor would be better able to meet with energy and force the Communist propaganda offensive and to initiate its own attack on behalf of the workers of the free world.

Lastly, the ICFTU might well consider new ways to improve its relations with the International Federation of Christian Trade Unions, which has important influence in many countries. The IFCTU now has about 2 million members. While the core of its strength continues to be in Europe, it also has offices or representatives in former French Africa, the Congo, Viet-Nam, and Chile. An important postwar decision of the IFCTU was to accept unions of workers "believing in God" rather than just Christian organizations. Thus it has included the Vietnamese Confederation of Christian Labor, most of whose members are Buddhist. While it has joined with the ICFTU in condemning the repression of trade-union rights in Spain and while important steps toward cooperation have been taken recently, relations between the two organizations are still distant. This is unfortunate because the IFCTU has a number of highly dedicated and effective trade-union leaders in the field who could be of the utmost help in any unified free labor effort. In addition, it has a strong ideological motivation which is important in fighting the ideology of communism, especially in the Catholic countries of Latin America.

Strengthening American Labor's Foreign Activity

American labor must face other facts. While it is without doubt the most respected segment of the American community in the developing world, while its great contribution to the welfare of American workers is admired, and its help to workers the world over is appreciated, there is no doubt that in many key areas it has been losing ground. Its prestige has suffered in some areas because while it has done a great deal, it has not been able to do enough, and at times it has unfortunately identified itself with the wrong people. Working too much through men at the top of the political ladder, it has failed to encourage enough of the young trade-union leaders at the lower levels who are destined to have an important place in future years. It has had neither the resources nor the men to be able to go for long periods of time to the fields and villages where the job must be done, and to assist in building strong, permanent, and responsible organizations at the local level. It has at times preached too much and done too little. Its failures have by no means all been its own fault. American management and our government must also share the blame. And the American people must always be grateful for the selfless devotion and real contribution of American labor and its dedicated leaders to the cause of freedom and democracy abroad.

To be more effective in accomplishing its international objectives American labor should, in my opinion, undertake certain new kinds of work, intensify some of its present activities, and expand and reorganize its international staff. A basic requirement is that there must be recognition, at the highest levels of American labor, of its importance to the fulfillment of United States foreign policy and of the precise role that labor is playing in the political as well as the economic development of the countries of Asia, Africa, and Latin America. New and intensive efforts should be made to clarify the development of AFL-CIO international policies and programs, and to ensure that the head of its International Affairs Department has the authority necessary for effective direction of these policies and programs. The current dissension between the AFL and CIO wings of the organization impedes effective concerted action and promotes confusion and bitterness in the labor movement itself, in government, and abroad. There may be reasons and justification for discord between the various segments of American labor on domestic matters, but there is no room for disunity in AFL-CIO foreign operations. Free labor has plenty of adversaries around the world without fighting itself. Strong leadership must be exercised to heal the breach between the AFL and CIO in international affairs. I realize fully that there are difficulties of substantial proportions in the way, some revolving around conflicting personalities; but they must be overcome before American labor is as effective abroad as it must be.

Every major American union should appoint at least one permanent staff member to handle international affairs. He would maintain liaison with his union's International Trade

Secretariat and the central AFL-CIO office. He would be responsible for initiative and planning in the international field, would recruit able young men from his union to serve abroad, receive and assist foreign trade-union visitors, and generally erect the basic structure necessary for fulfilling his union's responsibility for leadership abroad. Periodically the AFL-CIO should assemble the international directors of all major American unions to discuss international problems and develop policies and programs. These meetings should be concerned, too, with the policies pursued by American unions in their particular Trade Secretariats. The autonomy of the ITS and its American affiliate should not prevent coordination at a central point within the AFL-CIO. With a unified and strengthened International Affairs Department in the AFL-CIO, American labor would be able to act decisively and quickly, preferably through its affiliates in the Trade Secretariats. It could step up its recruitment of well-qualified trade-union leaders to serve abroad, working in the field to help organize and build strong, free, worker organizations. It could expand the pool of American labor technicians and officials who could be ready to answer quickly a government call to serve with a trade fair mission, help in an AID or Peace Corps project, or join the Foreign Service, temporarily or permanently, as a labor attaché. The AFL-CIO should expand programs to ensure that men who go abroad are well trained, linguistically and otherwise. Furthermore, the job security of these men should be preserved so that they are not deterred from serving abroad. Some of the most effective men we have working abroad for our government came from the American labor movement, but there are not enough of them and too frequently, in order to get the right men, high-level pressure has had to be used to persuade the American labor movement to let them go, and even then only after serious delays. I know from my own experience that there are quantities of good men in the American labor movement who are eager to serve abroad either with our trade unions, the Trade Secretariats, or as part of a governmental program. Unfortunately, however, there is far too little being done to recruit these men, train them and make them ready for immediate service abroad. The temptation to push the misfit at home into the international area, must, of course, be scrupulously resisted.

In general, American unions should be encouraged to increase their participation with the Trade Secretariats. The American labor movement should also seriously consider whether many of its unilateral activities in the developing world would not be better handled through the Trade Secretariats, as has been suggested earlier in this chapter. Given the suspicions which inevitably surround an American operating alone in some neutralist countries, given the reluctance of many good non-Communist worker leaders to accept help directly from the United States, given the risks of alienating our friends and allies in Europe, Great Britain, and elsewhere by "going it alone" in areas where they may feel a certain pride or right of jurisdiction, it might be better to work together through a Secretariat, in which American interests are protected and which can make the American worker's dollar go further and accomplish more.

Dealing with Foreign Unions

American labor with its free world allies must clarify the basis upon which it decides which unions do not merit recognition, encouragement, or support from the free world. At the same time it must know as precisely as possible what type of worker organization it wants to encourage. This judgment, which is essentially a political one, has an important bearing on the future success of free labor in the world struggle. Thus it is also of central importance to the fulfillment of U.S. foreign policy.

There is a wide measure of agreement that Sino-Soviet bloc worker organizations are not trade unions at all, but are part of the international Communist conspiracy and thus the enemies of freedom and social justice. They therefore should receive no recognition or encouragement. Despite the fact that increasing numbers of representatives from non-Communist labor are attending WFTU meetings and visiting Moscow and Peking, it would appear essential that free labor maintain its firm opposition to such recognition and do all in its power to discourage it.

Yugoslavia presents a slightly different problem. It has been the policy of the United States to invest large sums of money in the economic development of Yugoslavia. Our programs of aid and food distribution in Yugoslavia have been unusually successful and have helped greatly to preserve that country's independence from Moscow. Relations between the United States and Yugoslavia are generally satisfactory, but Yugoslavs are deeply offended by the refusal of American labor to visit their country or talk to their trade-union leaders. To be sure, while there are important differences between worker organizations in Yugoslavia and the U.S.S.R., they are both Communist. But in view of the importance to the free world and free labor of an independent Yugoslavia, might there not be justification for some differentiation in American labor's attitude toward Yugoslavia and that toward the bloc countries?

With respect to the United Arab Republic a third situation arises. Trade unions in the U.A.R. are firmly under the control of the government and yet they do play a significant part, not only in the economic and social development of the country, but also in improving the welfare of workers. American labor's attitude toward U.A.R. trade unions is somewhat obscure. The oil workers have excellent relations with the Egyptian oil workers' union, which is a member of the petroleum workers' ITS. Important segments of the American labor movement, however, are strongly committed to the Israeli workers' federation, Histadrut, and there is some question whether they are similarly eager to improve relations with Arab unions. It is important in this regard to remember that Egyptian worker organizations are vigorously non-Communist and are having an important influence in Africa. On many issues, such as Algerian freedom and colonialism, their views and those of the AFL-CIO are close. Perhaps it would be well to encourage more ITS to follow the good example of the oil workers in the U.A.R. so as to bring that country's unions more within the sphere of democratic influence.

Not only in their relations with Yugoslavia and Egypt, but in their activities throughout the underdeveloped world, American and European trade unions have to face the problem of political control of unions by parties or governments.

The degree of control varies considerably. In Ghana and Guinea, it is virtually complete; and yet, as we have seen, the trade unions of both of these countries are extremely important in the political development of Africa south of the Sahara today. They are used by their governments as international as well as domestic agencies for the promotion of national goals. Their leaders are high in the councils of government. It may be hard in some ways to differentiate the trade unions in Ghana and Guinea from the state tools of the Soviet bloc, but on the other hand it is important to remember that neither of these countries has jelled politically. They are not yet hard and fast dictatorships. They are changing and subject almost inevitably to continuing change in the years to come. Thus it is important for American labor, working preferably through the Secretariats, to maintain contact with worker organizations and their leaders in Ghana and Guinea and countries like them. It is important to help them in every way possible to strengthen their organizations in the hope that through strength may come a measure of independence, increasing respect for democracy, and dedication to maintaining their hard-won political freedom.

In Tunisia the trade unions are extensively intertwined with government and the Neo-Destour party, but, as we have seen, they have also developed considerable intrinsic strength through their economic cooperative endeavors. This strength is having several important effects. In the first place it is proving that a trade union can responsibly promote the interests of its members and at the same time contribute to the economic and social development of a less-developed country. Tunisian worker organizations are improving the democracy and stability of the country by providing a responsive outlet for grievances; and, while not fully independent of government, they are sufficiently powerful to have an influence both on government and on the economic life of the country in general. Thirdly, the UGTT is now strong enough to succeed in withstanding subversion and overthrow by the Communists or other outside forces and is becoming an important influence for freedom and democracy in Africa.

There are several reasons why governments in newly developing countries feel obliged to exert controls over labor organizations. Perhaps first is the need felt by leaders such as Nasser and Nkrumah to consolidate their political base, to obtain popular support for their policies, to prevent divisive elements in the society from weakening or destroying it, and to keep out Communist conspirators. There is also the need in almost all newly developing countries to devote a sizable share of the country's total production to its development; to force an austerity program which will ensure a maximum level of national saving. Some countries, therefore, may feel that they cannot allow worker organizations to become too powerful in their demands for a higher standard of living for their membership. All available funds are needed for the development of the country as a whole. One of the chief appeals of communism to leaders of developing countries is its ability to force saving. In Red China today, for example, about 23 per cent of the national income is saved for development purposes. In India the figure is only about 11 per cent, a rise of only 6 per cent from 1951. It is expected to reach 14 per cent by 1966.[9]

Either the government must compel this austerity or it must be democratically achieved, as India is trying to do. This poses a special problem for worker organizations, which traditionally have maintained the loyalty of their members and become strong by securing wage increases and other improvements for their members through collective bargaining, holding the strike as the ultimate weapon. Increasingly, trade unions are discovering that in a country that must undergo rapid development in order to survive, these traditional procedures may not be in either the union's or the country's best interests. They are perceiving in fact that there is a mutuality of interest between the nation and labor. A relatively simple solution would be to abolish trade unions and leave the economic system to the government as in totalitarian countries, but in doing so a number of other important characteristics of the society are lost. The economic systems become monolithic. Private initiative perishes. Democracy itself is eliminated. A monstrous and crippling bureaucratic pall spreads over the land. Furthermore, the seeds of revolution are planted by such suppression. History has shown many times that freedom rises from the ashes of dictatorship and often in the forefront are the worker organizations. So in order to keep a vigorous econ-

[9] Ward, cited, pp. 145, 146.

omy with room for maximum enterprise and initiative as well as a measure of democracy, nearly all of the newly developing countries recognize the vital role of worker organizations.

It is also evident that the role of these organizations is different and must be different from that of American and European labor today. In order to survive and meet the pressures of subversion they must be strong. To be strong they must maintain and expand membership loyalty. But in doing so, they cannot act in opposition to the national good. They cannot make irresponsible demands for gain out of proportion to the general gain. So it is that the example of trade unions in Tunisia and Israel, the railway workers in Indonesia, the Ahmedabad Textile Labor Association in India, among others, is of such compelling importance to the less-developed world today. Their example is also of vital importance to American labor and free labor everywhere and can serve as an important key to the achievement of the broad goals of U.S. foreign policy.

For worker organizations can indeed help their membership maintain its strength against subversion and, at the same time, become responsible and stabilizing elements in a nation, making an important contribution to national economic and social development. They are doing just this in the several countries I have mentioned. They are creating wealth, not merely dividing or distributing it. They are making cooperation and community organization and not detracting from them. Through that precious combination of ideals and ability, they are proving themselves to be constructive elements in the revolutionary pursuit of freedom and social justice.

I do not mean to say that worker organizations should abandon collective bargaining, or should in any way weaken the vigor with which they press for a fair distribution of existing wealth. An austerity program for national saving can never be effective unless all elements in the community share equally in it. People will only sacrifice if the burden of sacrifice is justly shared by all. If the rich are getting richer while the poor become poorer, then, of course, no austerity program will work. The workers cannot be expected to have in mind the national interest if their employers do not share the same enlightenment. As long as some people in less-developed countries can afford to import cars from the United States at a cost of $20,000 or more, the worker is going to drive with all the power he can muster for an increase in his pitiful wage. Workers should and will accept austerity for the whole country but not for themselves alone. As the total wealth of a nation increases, it is the vital function of a worker organization to ensure its fair distribution through the processes of collective bargaining. But while the squeeze is on, while the money barrel is still very shallow, it must have other means of maintaining and protecting itself.

There has been much discussion of the relations of trade unions with political parties. Many traditionalists within the American labor movement have decried the umbilical attachment which, they say, reduces the trade unions in many countries to feeble adjuncts of the party, susceptible to corruption and political machination and incapable of the intrinsic strength necessary to meet Communist aggression. We can all agree that a union must have intrinsic strength to perform its function and meet the challenge of freedom. We in America would argue that this strength is best acquired by independence from the government or any political party. This is surely sound for us. But in Britain, Europe, Scandinavia and Israel, for example, there are strong trade unions, admirably fulfilling the purposes of democracy, and yet allied to political parties. It has been traditional for the political parties in these countries to look to trade unions for their base of mass appeal. In most of these countries, however, the unions preceded the political parties. This is an important distinction. The unions built a strength of their own which they then shared with political parties in order to accomplish their purposes in society.

In the underdeveloped countries, however, the unions generally grew as adjuncts to and agents for the political parties. They serve a variety of political, social, and economic purposes. In India, for example, INTUC from the start has been in many ways a tool for the Congress party. Its paucity of leadership, lack of funds, and the enormity of the challenge it faces have kept it subservient to the political leaders of the party. As we have seen, it was used as a tool in combating a government workers' strike. It is losing ground to the Communists and is badly split from the other non-Communist federation, HMS (see page 42). Some say INTUC must sever its relations with the Congress party to gain strength and meet the Communist menace. This is an oversimplification. INTUC cannot conceivably cut its political ties until it has the strength to do so. It would collapse if it attempted to and the situation would be worse than at present. The Congress party provides important leadership, protection and resources, which, in its weakened condition, INTUC needs to survive. So there is no point in glibly preaching about the evils of a trade union affiliating with a political party.

The real need is for INTUC to strengthen itself and for the Congress party, in effect the Indian government, to assist it actively in this effort. How can this be done?

First, INTUC should look to its strongest element, the Ahmedabad Textile Labor Association. This union has been a strong constructive force in Indian society for more than twenty years. It has provided its members not only with a relatively high standard of living, regularly increasing wages, and vastly improved working conditions, but it has, through cooperation, built schools, hospitals, clinics, and housing. It has instituted various pension and insurance programs for the protection of its membership, and has in general raised their lot far above the Indian average. At the same time, it carries on vigorous collective bargaining with textile employers for further benefits.

Why has this example not been followed elsewhere in India? A major reason, as we saw in Chapter II, is the small number of men and women capable of leadership. Politicians and others, without the capacity of Mahatma Gandhi and the other great leaders of Ahmedabad, took hold of INTUC operations in other parts of the country and the results have been less than satisfactory. Now INTUC is sending its young men, trained at Ahmedabad, out into the field to take over young organizations, and there is hope for the future. But INTUC will need great help. It will need help in training its young leaders to organize and build a union, to start cooperative enterprises, to build schools and hospitals, to keep books, and administer a vast civic enterprise such as that at Ahmedabad.

The opportunities are many. Perhaps most outstanding is the new steel industry of India mentioned earlier. I have visited these new steel plants. They are extremely impressive, ultramodern factories built in the jungles of Bihar and Orissa. The British, Germans, and Soviets each built a plant. It was interesting to see how remarkably superior the Russians were in establishing good community and industrial relations with the Indian construction workers compared to either the British or the Germans. They lived with the Indian workers in an enormous compound which they built. Their children went to school with Indian children. They built hospitals and clinics. They provided movies several times a week—American and British films as well as Russian. The British and Germans were there strictly to get a job done and in the meantime to live as comfortably as possible. I heard a story of one Russian who had a few too many vodkas one night. He was immediately shipped home and all alcohol was forbidden on the project, an important appreciation of the sensibilities of teetotaling Indians. Be that as it may, these plants now constitute the industrial heart of India. Their control by forces sympathetic with India's freedom and democracy is essential. Communist leaders have designated their work forces as prime targets for subversion. This represents a critical test of INTUC and HMS strength. Can they together meet the challenge? This is perhaps one of the most vital questions in India today.

Here is an ideal opportunity for INTUC to extend the example of Ahmedabad, organize the workers in their jungle factories, collect dues from them, however small, in order to give them a sense of unity and participation, build cooperative housing, build schools and hospitals, start a pension and insurance fund, and make the workers proud and conscious of their union. It is an opportunity to force upon them the realization that the Communists are not only representatives of an external power but in making their violent, pie-in-the-sky appeals for higher and higher wages, regardless of the effect on the country as a whole, they are in fact national traitors. Free labor can show Indian workers that a democratic union can meet the essential needs of the worker, can represent his legitimate interests with the employer, but at the same time can do so in an entirely patriotic way, contributing to his welfare as well as the nation's by organizing cooperative endeavors.

American labor can help enormously here, especially through the Trade Secretariats, by providing funds, technical assistance, leadership training, and moral support for such ventures. But in a larger sense it is not really money that is needed from the United States or anywhere else. It is Indian leadership itself that must make INTUC come alive and preserve the freedom of India's steel industry. In order that this leadership may arise and be successful the

Indian government, the Congress party, and India's free labor movement must clearly see the need and the problem.

Relations between a union and a political party are not necessarily good or bad, in and of themselves. In some countries a close relationship may be unavoidable and protests against it only serve as an indicator of lack of understanding of political realities. In others a severance of the relationship may invite Communist subversion. Frequently such close ties are the effect rather than the cause of weakness, and the unfortunate consequences can be mitigated by providing a means for giving the union intrinsic strength.

Some go farther and argue that in order to contribute to the social and economic development of the country a worker organization must have the cooperation if not the assistance, of government or the ruling party. This is largely true, owing to the pervasive role that governments necessarily play in newly developing societies. The argument goes on to contend that cooperation leads to even closer ties between the government or political party and the union, with a consequent weakening of the latter. This is not necessarily true. Certainly Tunisian labor's economic activities have neither increased nor lessened its ties to government. It was under government control before. If anything, it is becoming less so because of its increasing intrinsic strength. In India, it is hard to conceive of INTUC becoming any more subservient to Congress leaders, no matter what happens. The danger is that it will be beaten in the race with the Communists. Cooperation of Congress leaders in increasing INTUC's economic activities would strengthen it and give it the basis from which it quite conceivably could stand more on its own legs.

American labor should, therefore, reconsider any preconceptions it may have about the rights and wrongs of trade unionism in less-developed countries. It must look at the problems of each country and each organization separately and seek clear, uncluttered judgments on what is the best, most effective, and most practical way to meet the needs of workers, given their particular situation at a particular time. In so doing, it should always keep in mind that whatever may be the ideal relationship between government or a political party and a trade union, the immediate need is to encourage the development of a total society which will be able to withstand subversion, maintain its freedom, and establish a stable political and economic base upon which democracy and social justice can be built.

American labor should look into its own past at the time of our Revolution and find the similarities and historical bonds which tie us from those days to the peoples of the new countries today. European workers also should recall that in the nineteenth and early twentieth centuries they built cooperatives for the protection of their membership and for the general good. Free labor should encourage in every way possible the development of soundly conceived, well-administered economic and social cooperative efforts on the part of worker organizations in the developing countries for the benefit not only of their membership but of their nation as a whole. Simultaneously and as the situation changes, free labor will also be able to assist in the development of strong, responsible, collective bargaining systems to ensure the fair distribution of existing wealth.

In such a way reform can come without revolt and economic growth can mean true progress. Permanent structures will be built into the new societies which will help to strengthen the fragile fabric of freedom against the awful efficiency of tyranny.

Chapter V

THE CHALLENGE TO AMERICAN BUSINESS

American labor is by no means the only group in our country with an interest in the affairs of worker organizations abroad; nor is it the only group whose foreign operations have a direct bearing on U.S. foreign policy. American management has, if anything, a greater cause for concern and a greater obligation to review its policies and practices, having in mind the special importance of foreign labor organizations, not only to the continued well-being of American companies overseas, but also to the achievement of our national aims.

It has become urgent that United States business put new emphasis on its good conduct abroad, particularly in the newly developing countries. The vital role of many worker organizations and their leaders in Asia, Africa, and Latin America gives special significance to the industrial relations of American companies in those areas. Labor leaders are no longer—if they ever were—obscure, no-accounts who can be treated casually as just another problem in foreign operations. For good or evil, they are presidents or future presidents, the friends of presidents, the power behind thrones and parties, or the leaders of revolution.

Today it is clearer than ever that neither American companies nor the U.S. government can afford reckless, exploitative, and ignorant policies—or the appearance of them—which would give plausibility to the demagogue's cry of "economic imperialism." Whether it likes it or not every American company abroad flies the flag of the United States. To the people who work for it, who live around it, who come in contact with it in any way, it is America. This is an awesome responsibility.

The peoples of the less-developed world are insisting on a better way of life. They are investigating which of the various systems, procedures, and techniques for development are the most effective. To be sure, they are concerned for their liberty, their freedom, and the dignity of their people, but uppermost in the minds of many of the leaders of the new world is the urgent and primary need for quick economic development and an improvement in the standard of living of their people. In filling this need, they quite naturally want to keep for themselves as much of the benefit of industrialization as possible. As Clarence B. Randall put it:

> The eager young leaders in the underdeveloped areas have little desire to share with anyone, least of all foreigners, the responsibility for improving the lot of their people. They are swayed by those who say that while the United States is undoubtedly a great country, a new nation cannot wait for the evolutionary process of private initiative but should follow instead the shortcut methods of the Soviets. The warning that this involves loss of personal freedom falls on deaf ears. Yet such leaders are usually highly intelligent and their attitudes can be changed if their experience with American private enterprise is favorable.[1]

[1] "How to Get Along Overseas," *The Atlantic,* March 1959.

We are proud of our heritage of private initiative. We believe our economic system to be the most efficient and productive in the world, and we can show that it has brought an unprecedented measure of social justice to the American people. But the fact that it has worked for us is no proof that it will work in countries whose history, problems, and needs are entirely different. The peoples of the newly developing world are waiting for evidence that American management practices and techniques and our free economic system, which places a heavy emphasis on private initiative, are in fact useful for them. It is not enough to show that our procedures result in high production and great efficiency. We must also prove that American business is conscious of the fact that material accomplishment is unsatisfactory unless it allows the fulfillment of those higher ends of social justice, individual dignity, and true democracy which we say we value above all else. To those who say: "What about profits for the stockholders?" I would say there is no choice. Either we are true to our own highest principles or we will fail, as businessmen, as labor leaders, as a people, and as a nation. And if we fail, of course, there will be no profits.

The Place of U.S. Investment Abroad

American management has an important and growing role in the development of the economies of less-developed countries, especially Latin America. U.S. direct private investments abroad at the beginning of 1961 were valued at nearly $33 billion, more than four and a half times what they were immediately after World War II. Much of the increase was in Canada and Europe, but the figures for underdeveloped countries are substantial. In Latin America, U.S. investment went from slightly more than $3 billion in

1946 to more than $9 billion in 1960, in Asia and Africa from less than $500 million to over $3 billion.[2]

Impressive as these figures are, they become more so when we remember that American enterprise abroad brings with it much more than money. It places a reasonably permanent institution in the country in which it locates. This can be an important source of stability and progress, or it can be a cause for revolt and ruin.

American foreign enterprise not only supplies badly needed and generally welcome capital for development but also provides a useful example of industrial techniques and practices which may be of lasting value to underdeveloped countries. The American system of collective bargaining and labor-management relations, while not applicable everywhere to the same degree, can be of crucial importance to the smooth and peaceful transition of a rural society into an industrial one. It is interesting to note that in many areas of the world where American management is established, collective bargaining is most advanced. Many companies have performed a real service to the cause of peace and freedom by showing exploitative local employers that enlightened labor-management relations can increase efficiency and production as well as political stability and community happiness. If we are interested in encouraging private initiative, then it becomes vital to show how private enterprise can meet the needs of a newly developing country that seeks both rapid economic development and an increasing measure of social justice for its people.

There are many fine examples of American companies which have contributed a great deal to the countries in which they have located, practicing the best and most enlightened principles of domestic U.S. business, building

[2] U.S. Department of Commerce, Office of Business Economics, *U.S. Business Investments in Foreign Countries* (Washington: GPO, 1960), pp. 1-6; *Survey of Current Business*, August 1961.

respect and understanding for our country and our way of life. I have seen their good work in India, in the U.A.R., in Nigeria, where American industrialists have gone, often at considerable personal sacrifice, and stayed year after year, assisting these countries in their growth, building the skills of their people, respecting the dignity of the worker and his right to a fair share of the fruits of his labor, regardless of his race or his color or his economic status. I know of many other such examples in Asia and Latin America.

This, of course, is not charitable work. These companies are doing well, making money for their stockholders, and building their capital investment; but they are doing it with a broad sense of responsibility, in such a way as to make them partners with the people in national development rather than adversaries. They are sailing with the winds of change instead of against them. They are spreading their ownership as far as possible among nationals of the countries in which they do business. They take no doctrinaire view about what role government should play. They take the situation as it is, try to understand and work in harmony with it. They readily accept the necessity of recognizing and encouraging strong non-Communist trade unions in their own interests as well as in those of the United States and the countries where they have invested.

It is perhaps unfair to single out particular companies for praise because many deserve it, but a few examples may be useful. In Venezuela, Bethlehem and U.S. Steel have seen the advantage of enlightened labor policies even though these have resulted in keeping the labor cost per worker employed by these corporations in Venezuela above that on the Mesabi Range of Minnesota. The United Steelworkers of America has gone abroad with our steel companies and has helped build extremely strong and effective unions in the steel and iron industry of many developing countries. These unions have negotiated collective agreements with their employers, equal in scope and benefits to many contracts in the United States or Europe. Similarly, Creole Petroleum Corporation, a subsidiary of Standard Oil of New Jersey, has an excellent record in Venezuela. It is building comfortable individual homes which it is selling to the workers on reasonable terms and financing at low interest rates. They are building modern communities in the oil fields with community centers, churches, and playgrounds to replace the old "company towns." The influence as well as affluence of the Venezuelan oil unions is evident in the impressive new headquarters built by the Federation of Petroleum Workers in Caracas, in which, incidentally, the Venezuelan oil employers' association leases two floors. The union conducts training classes in this building, students being sent by their locals with all expenses paid.

The American Bauxite Company in Jamaica also has negotiated excellent contracts with its workers and has increased wages about 400 per cent in recent years. General Electric, Squibb, Minneapolis-Honeywell, Kaiser Aluminum, and the Grace Company all have good records in Latin America also. While some have been paternalistic, all have dealt fairly with trade unions and contributed to the welfare of the communities where they are located. Many of these companies and others have also gone a long way to bring in local managers and partners and to spread their ownership throughout the country. A striking example of what can be done along these lines is provided by a British firm, the United Africa Company, a subsidiary of Unilever. Engaged in a wide variety of trading and other activities in a large number of countries, UAC has for decades followed a policy of hiring, training, and promoting Africans. The company runs management training institutes and has done a great deal to encourage local industrialization, investing as a minority stockholder in a number of enterprises making everything from face powder to building materials. It has cooperated with the governments of the newly independent countries of Africa and established its branches as, for example, Ghanaian and Nigerian corporations.

Companies that follow such policies are in many ways the most effective ambassadors we can have. In helping themselves, they render a great service to democracy, foreign policy, and the free economic system. They deserve the gratitude of all Americans. Unfortunately, however, there are also companies—a minority—who have left their finer traditions at home and sought maximum short-run profits by extracting what they could at the expense of their own prestige and that of the United States. Taking advantage of feudal economic conditions that still exist in many developing countries, the weakness of worker organizations, and their own overwhelming economic strength, some American companies have retarded progress and given much comfort to the enemies of freedom. Sometimes in collusion with a ruling oligarchy or a government fearful of losing U.S. investment dollars, they have deliberately sought to crush trade unions and have disregarded the needs of the people in whose country they operate. Since it is these companies that present the problems, they will occupy our attention for the rest of this chapter, to the exclusion of the others—the majority—whose policies are not open to fundamental objections.

One must recognize at the outset that even the most enlightened American company is at a disadvantage in many foreign countries. Francisco R. Lima, Ambassador to the United States from El Salvador, has described some prevalent Latin American attitudes toward U.S. private investment:

It is currently believed and felt in Latin America that the Latin American population has been and still is exploited by some unscrupulous foreign businessmen; that American firms established in Latin America are not interested in the well being of the local population nor in the economic development of these countries; that American businessmen including the home office executives, the local managers, foreign supervisors and foremen are often arrogant and discriminatory; that the economic development of the countries has been retarded by American investments because they have organized their business in such a way as to maintain these countries as suppliers of cheap raw materials or at the most as suppliers of cheap semi-finished products for the benefit of the American undertakings established in the United States or in other parts of the world; that the main objectives of foreign capital investing abroad is to find a market for surplus capital looking for higher profits and cheaper labor. . . . If to these purely economic factors we add the belief that army-supported dictators are also supported by the huge American monopolies, which thus have been able to obtain better and more favorable concessions for their undertakings, we would see how in the minds of the Latin American population even the unpopular dictatorships are attributed to American businessmen.[3]

Though these criticisms are largely unwarranted, unfair, and inaccurate, nevertheless there is little doubt that they reflect widely held views in underdeveloped countries. An anti-Communist trade-union leader from an important Latin American country recently said to me, about American management in his country: "They look down their noses at us and set themselves up in their own private communities." He cited a walled and gated portion of a Central American city where U.S. company personnel live in relative splendor, quite apart from those in whose country they are guests. He also complained that U.S. companies have in the past supported and sustained dictatorships in Latin America and he felt that they would like to see them back.

[3] "U.S. Management and Latin America," *Advanced Management*, January 1961.

In fact, he said, it has not been uncommon for some American companies to buy full-page advertisements praising the works of dictators in several Latin American countries.

A questionnaire sent to five hundred MIT alumni who are residents or natives of sixteen Latin American countries showed that while "U.S. companies are becoming increasingly identified with and accepted by the Latin American community," there is room for improvement.[4] In the eyes of many Latin Americans the primary concern of U.S. managers is the advancement of their own often narrowly conceived self-interest. An Argentine said: "Their sole objective is to make money and go home." A Chilean: "They want to make money in a country where taxes allow you to keep it." And a Panamanian: "The usual characteristics of an American businessman are an air of superiority and an attitude that to deal with him you must speak English. This is the general opinion." A Brazilian described the American businessman in his country as follows: "He thinks that only what is American is reliable. He feels that he is Santa Claus with his investment capital and know-how. He endeavors to convert people to the American way of life rather than to adapt to his foreign environment. He complains bitterly and tactlessly about local inefficiencies and errors, sounding as if he were the first to notice them, forgetting that if my children are ugly, I don't like outsiders to point it out to me."

A sixty-year-old Argentine general manager took a somewhat less hostile view:

The typical American businessman is capable, a good organizer, affable and has a good sense of humor. As in the United States, he maintains strict office hours and does not take time out for rest or relaxation. This is unlike his Latin American

[4] Michael H. Payson, *A Study of the Adjustment of United States Industry to the Environment of Latin America,* submitted to the School of Industrial Management of MIT, February 1961, as an M.S. thesis.

counterpart, who takes his business problems in a more personal way, keeping less regular but more extensive hours, often working in the intimacy of his home.

As an employer the American gets along well with his subordinates. They work in an environment of collaboration rather than "slavery," participating in the management of an industry which they are prone to feel will benefit the inhabitants of the country.

Socially the American businessman in Argentina attempts to gain the most comfort and diversion that his higher salary allows. For example, he tries to find housing which is modern and comfortable by American standards and is willing to pay exorbitant rents to get it, particularly if it is in an American community. Frequently American wives compete to see who can purchase the most expensive luxuries, articles which they would probably never buy in the United States. Such extravagance makes an extremely unfavorable impression on local people.

Americans seem perfectly willing to support private primary and secondary schools for their children. They are maintained so that their children can meet the admission requirements of U.S. universities; but because of them the opportunity is missed of learning local customs and habits from our children which might have resulted in a better understanding of mutual cultural and economic problems in the future.

The American businessman is exclusive. Most of his entertaining is done with other Americans, more often in the home than in local sporting or social clubs (where natives often are unwelcome). He is adept at organizing cocktail parties but rarely invites guests outside his circle.

His interest in cultural events here is limited to the commentary provided by his countrymen. He often goes to the movies and at times to the opera. He never goes to a local theater if the play is performed in Spanish. This is because of his poor knowledge of the language. When he arrives here he takes several lessons but when he can understand and be understood he drops them. As a result he rarely reads books by native authors, losing the great opportunity to acquaint himself with the manner of thinking of cultivated men in this country.[5]

Unreasonable as many of these criticisms are as generalizations, the behavior of some American businessmen justifies this kind of complaint. To be sure, also, American businessmen are not alone in being a target of such strictures. Similar things have been said for years about many of our government officials abroad. So far as support for dictatorial regimes is concerned, that too has sometimes been the practice of the U.S. government. In some cases, there has seemed to be no choice for the businessman. It would be asking a lot of an American manager in a foreign country to expect him to lean against the wind when our government is leaning with it. Moreover, it can be difficult to decide just how an American firm should combine the idea of effectively representing democratic ways with the desirability of conforming to the conditions of the foreign country in which it is located if that country is a dictatorship.

Labor Policy of American Companies Abroad

Policy toward labor is only one of an American firm's problems in an underdeveloped country but it is the one with which we are primarily concerned here.[6] It is a very important one, as I have already pointed out. And it is a very difficult one because it involves not just the cost of doing business or the economic welfare of the workers, but all the political, social, psychological, and ideological factors that give rise to the suspicion and hostility reflected in the attitudes just cited. Because of these complexities, even

---

[5] Same, pp. 20, 21.

[6] The people responding to Payson's questionnaire put their main emphasis on the quality and character of U.S. employees sent to Latin America; financial participation by Latin Americans in U.S. enterprises; the employment of Latin Americans in high positions and their opportunities for advancement.

desirable policies may have features that give offense; a simple decision on one matter may inadvertently have bad effects on another.

Very often American companies pay higher wages than local employers, provide better working conditions, and establish a wide variety of public services in the community which were not there before, such as schools and hospitals, even railroads and hotels. But in too many cases the good which the company may do is offset by bad personnel policies, anti-union activity, or discrimination in employment, promotion, housing, schooling, and a variety of other matters. And, of course, the houses and hospitals which the company builds usually belong to it and not to the workers. This is a distinction to consider when we remember the importance of ownership in the free system we are seeking to encourage.

Although some companies make a careful study of labor matters and particularly of the labor supply that will be available to them, too many American companies establish themselves in less-developed countries without sufficient research and analysis of these matters. Once in the field, they may be surprised and dismayed to find a lot of diseased and ignorant peasants, unskilled and unequipped to do what is expected of them. Furthermore, they find unanticipated labor-political difficulties which cause unreasonable bitterness and discouragement. They often neglect to consider the effects of local diseases and undernourishment on the productivity of the labor force, and frequently pay insufficient attention to local customs, superstitions, and emotional factors which can be of overriding importance. Even those who pay attention to these matters rarely make use of all the information available to them. The Bureau of International Labor Affairs, of which I was in charge for several years, maintains complete current information on labor developments and trade-union personalities around the world. With great care and competence the Bureau compiles country studies, which are generally unclassified and available for the asking. During my years in Washington only three employers asked for this information. As far as I know there is no other place in or out of government where such information can be found.

In many cases the home office lays down enlightened principles of labor relations and equips the local manager with quantities of good advice on personnel practices. But at the same time it may require unreasonable levels of production or profits from him, causing him to throw aside its good advice in the interest of meeting production quotas. Frequently, also, overseas managers and supervisors are chosen on the basis of their performance in the United States without sufficient regard for the entirely different set of problems they must confront abroad. A first-class manager in Detroit may well be a dismal failure in the Latin American jungle. In addition, many field men have been abroad too long. They have grown unaware of or callous to the revolutionary changes taking place around them, and have an unfortunate tendency to attribute all unsettling developments to "the Commies." It should be noted in passing that some American ambassadors have been equally shortsighted.

The myth of cheap labor in many newly developing countries has led some companies to forgo the trouble and expense of training to improve skills and increase productivity. An American manager may say to himself: "Why worry about raising skill levels and improving plant efficiency when we are making money now and the source of cheap labor appears inexhaustible?" He ignores the effects of such a policy on the dignity of the workers concerned, many of whom are vitally interested in advancement and determined to establish the basis of a better life for their children than that which they have suffered.

An American manager who adopts such a degrading and static attitude toward his workers and endeavors to build high profits by maintaining a mass of cheap labor is conforming to the Marxian description of "the capitalist." He is clouding his own true image and betraying the American industrial credo which revolutionized the capitalist system in the United States and defied Marx's predictions. For in the United States we have discovered that in the long run prosperity and growth cannot come piecemeal, enriching one segment of society at the expense of another. The manager prospers only as the worker prospers. We have come to realize that increasing productivity and plant efficiency make possible higher wages and lower prices, which in turn allow the workers to buy more and thus form a mass consumer market. It is on the basis of mass consumption that we have produced the most vigorous economic system in the world. It is so obviously in the interests of American enterprise as well as of the United States generally to transport abroad this aspect of our industrial revolution that it hardly seems worth mentioning. And yet some managers apparently cling to the outmoded nineteenth-century concept of high profits based on cheap labor and low productivity, with disastrous results. They fail to see the long-term advantage to all in building the purchasing power of the workers in newly developing countries, and are apparently unaware of the violent consequences of attempting to frustrate insistent demands for a better way of life. While clearly some countries are too small and too poor to offer new markets in the near future, the recent development of free trade areas and common markets in Latin America and elsewhere will surely open the door for more marketing activity on the part of enterprising producers.

Indeed, the concept of "cheap labor" is becoming more and more of a myth as wage rates continue their inevitable rise. For example, the case study made by the National

Planning Association of the Grace Company's experience in Peru reads:

> . . . although wages are low, labor costs are high in Peruvian industrial enterprises. Grace officials suggest, and we are inclined to agree with them, that over-all labor costs are no lower in their Lima mills than in most North American textile mills, despite the fact that the take-home pay of the average textile worker in Peru is scarcely one-third that of his counterpart in the United States. The experience of the manufacturing industries of Peru demonstrates quite conclusively that cheap labor does not usually result in lower labor costs. . . .[7]

The problem of the American manager abroad is heightened and complicated by the fact that generally he associates with the wealthiest local employers, many of whom still operate according to the dicta of nineteenth-century exploitative capitalism and who want to maintain cheap labor as the basis for their inordinately high profits. Some employers of Latin America, Asia, and Africa are apt to brand as communism any sort of social reform aimed at a more just distribution of wealth and a more equitable economic order. The American manager may find it difficult to disassociate himself from local employers of this type in whose country club he is welcomed and with whom he plays golf, but he must do so. It is one thing for an Indian, for example, to exploit other Indians, but it is quite a different thing for an American to do so. The American abroad must maintain a strong sense of his own roots, of his nation's purpose, of American values and principles. We cannot preach one thing and practice another and expect to have the world believe us.

Bribery presents the same kind of problems. Often it is

[7] Eugene W. Burgess and Frederick H. Harbison, *Casa Grace in Peru,* Second Case Study of *United States Business Performance Abroad* (Washington: National Planning Association, 1954), p. 70. One American mining company in Chile pays its workers an average of $280-$330 a month, with skilled technicians earning as much as $480.

taken for granted that American companies abroad must pay off local politicians because that is the way business is done in that part of the world. The local employers do it; it is accepted and understood. Times are changing, however, and whereas the people may forgive one of their own, they will often not forgive a foreigner. Frequently the price of bribery is too high, not only in the concessions to foreigners that result but in loss of national pride; and the people blame the tempter more than the tempted. Workers in a less-developed country have some right to expect an American manager to act according to his, and perhaps their, idea of what the United States stands for. If the manager fails to approximate this image, by bribery or in other ways, the damage he has done spreads, like the ripples on a pond, far beyond him and his company.

Management and Unions

In relations with workers' organizations abroad, there are a distressing number of instances in which U.S. management has weakened the democratic forces and strengthened the Communists.

First of all, it is necessary to understand that Communist trade-union leaders in the newly developing countries, as in those that are industrially advanced, are particularly clever in their approach to labor-management relations. They are capable of disregarding any aspect of Marxist-Leninist doctrine to further their immediate ends. I have had many employers in Asia and Latin America tell me, for example, that it is much easier for them to do business with Communist trade unions than with the non-Communists. The Communists have better control over their membership. Union discipline is greater. They generally do what they promise. They live up to their contracts and are solicitous in their understanding of management's problems. This may all be quite true, of course, until the moment comes when the time is right for upheaval and overthrow. Then, as we have seen in a number of countries, the highly disciplined Communist organizations rise up and contracts, agreements, and understandings go out the window. The once-satisfied manager finds himself flat out, his plant expropriated or destroyed, and his country embarrassed.

It is hard to believe that successful businessmen can have such naïveté about Communist means and objectives, and yet in several Latin American countries that I know of an American company has apparently gone out of its way to weaken and destroy non-Communist worker unions, only to have them replaced by militant Communist organizations, which, although perhaps momentarily cooperative, gravely jeopardize not only the company's future but the country's freedom. In an effort to avoid any union at all, some companies have played a free union off against its Communist competitor. The result is too frequently a victory for the Communist union because of its superior financial support, discipline, and organizational strength.

This is a particularly serious problem in small countries where an American company may control a substantial percentage of the national economy. If a Communist-led union can gain control of the work force of this company, it can, relying on funds from Havana or Moscow, quite conceivably strike for a sufficiently long period to put the company out of business. Thus in one stroke the company would be wiped out, the nation's economy crippled, the political regime toppled, and a highly disciplined organization with a broad popular base put in a position to assume control, subject to orders from Moscow.

There are a wide variety of examples of anti-union activity by American companies abroad. An American company in Peru has steadfastly refused to allow its workers to organize, using armed guards when necessary. The company says that any organization would inevitably fall under Communist domination, neglecting to realize that its current policies could not be better designed to serve Communist ends. Another in Singapore for many years fought efforts by the ICFTU to build a strong worker organization in resistance to serious Communist pressure in that city.

Some U.S. companies provide the communities in which they operate with a vast array of public services, including hospitals, schools, housing, transportation, and recreation facilities. They are legitimately proud of these contributions to the better life of their workers and their families. But too often they make the mistake of thinking that such services can be a substitute for good labor-management relations, for the recognition of the right of workers to organize a strong trade union, and the obligation of the company to bargain with this union. They fail to see that the dignity of the worker is at stake. He may be grateful for paternalistic services. They help him and his family emerge from misery. But he is insistent about his right to be treated as an individual with a legitimate claim to self-reliance. His trade union becomes a symbol of dignity and when it is smashed he feels a personal blow.

Not everyone in the underdeveloped countries sees unions this way. On balance, there is little doubt that the cause of freedom is damaged far more by the bad labor practices of local businessmen, who are natives of a developing country, than by foreign managers. Were we to succeed in placing all American foreign entrepreneurs on the side of the angels, the threat of communism would still be very real unless they were joined by the entrepreneurs of the home country. This makes the position of the American firm abroad particularly difficult. And it complicates one's judgment about otherwise desirable courses of action. Some American companies in Latin America are exploring ways of divesting themselves of parts of their holdings, to permit

Latin Americans to take them over. This seems a sound way of permitting local interests to share in the development the American firm has brought. But it can have dangerous elements. Suppose, for example, that the U.S. company is a large one; its workers are members of a strong, well-organized, democratic trade union. Then some of the company's holdings are turned over to local employers. Many of them have little use for strong trade unions. Under the country's laws the division of the property into relatively small parcels makes it legally possible to avoid dealing with trade unions. The result of the move to bring in local interests is to weaken the trade unions of the country. In a small country they might be destroyed and the principal force capable of resisting Communist subversion removed.

American management must draw a very sharp distinction between what its labor problems are in the United States and what they are abroad. It should be quite clear in its own mind that the policies and techniques it uses to meet those problems must be quite different. Neither consciously nor subconsciously should it confuse a trade union in the United States with one in Ecuador, India, or Nigeria. American management must be keenly aware that while it may accept a union in the United States as a bothersome fact of life or as a worthy adversary, it must regard a strong, democratic, militant worker organization in a less-developed country as useful for the survival of its enterprise. It must see such an organization as its hope for evolving a stable economic relationship in the country, protecting it against political upheaval and expropriation as well as preserving the country against Communist subversion. It is insufficient for the American manager in Latin America, for example, simply to countenance a local labor union. It is worse still for him to seek to buy off the leaders or to shop around for the "softest" union and do business with it; needless to say, it is even worse to accept the hypocritically offered, and sham, security and discipline often proffered by Communist-controlled worker organizations as any kind of promise for long-term successful labor-management relations or political stability.

The American industrialist must convince himself that it is for his own long-term good to assist in building a stable economic institution in the community in the form of a sound, fairly balanced collective bargaining structure. He must see that this will protect him from many of the ills with which he is now beset.

At present in many instances when a worker or his union has a grievance against an American company, he lacks the strength and technical skills to prevail in what in the United States would be a normal grievance or collective bargaining procedure. He thus goes to his political party or to the government with a request that a law be passed to help him out of his difficulty. Often a law is passed, frequently not a very practical one, and the company and all other companies find themselves hobbled by one more complicated and bothersome regulation.

If the worker or his union is not satisfied by the political and legislative action taken as a result of his grievance, he is obviously easy prey for the irresponsible and hypocritical Communist agitator and may well join his cause. If this situation happens often enough and is serious enough, a number of consequences may follow. The labor movement becomes Communist-dominated, union antagonism increases, and companies face the threat of work stoppage, violence, and eventually political upheaval. If the grievances are sufficiently widespread and the government does not meet them, the government may be overthrown and American companies confronted by imminent expulsion or expropriation. We have seen this drama acted out in a number of countries in Latin America, the Middle East, and Asia with distressing regularity.

A very different history might follow if the American company came to a developing country with the policy and the desire to deal with a strong, free union that could represent its employees responsibly, vigorously, and effectively. It would then try to find ways to encourage a democratic union, preferably already on the scene, to develop the techniques and skills necessary to build itself into an effective collective bargaining agent.

One way in which an American company abroad might encourage loyalty to the union among the workers and strengthen it against external pressures, would be to channel social development work through the union. For example, many companies in less-developed countries provide housing for their employees, particularly if they are located far from an urban center. As a result the company frequently faces the traditional difficulties of the "company town." There is friction with the fringe community of shopkeepers and hawkers, and countless gripes among workers who feel unfairly treated. Some suspect that failure to get better quarters is a punishment for lack of subservience. The housing problem might be lifted from the company's back and at the same time the free, democratic union could be strengthened if the provision of workers' housing were made a union responsibility under a collective bargaining agreement giving the union funds, administrative personnel, and technical assistance. This step would give a worker more of a proprietary interest in his house; arrangements might be worked out whereby he could eventually own it. There could be no better antidote to communism than this. Similar actions could be taken by the company to encourage and assist the union in establishing cooperatives, building and loan associations, hospitals, clinics, schools, and recreation facilities.

If such a course were followed, the company would have developed a stable economic relationship with a strong union capable of meeting the needs of the workers; established a sound community capable of resisting political upheaval; and it would have shown a good example of how economic democracy works. If by chance the country underwent political change or revolution, the company would be in a reasonably good position to withstand any consequent pressures.

Such a course will not always be open to a company, or it may not appear practicable. The local legal situation may prevent it; the government may block offers to strengthen the union; the union may lack the strength and administrative capacity to play its part, and perhaps even the wish to take this kind of responsibility. My sketch is not a prescription but an example of the kinds of possibilities American companies ought to explore. Their willingness to do this and their active leadership in helping to make these and other possibilities real are the important things. They must be careful not to create company unions. When they can take these steps in response to union requests they will be better off than if they have to take all the initiative.

While the course of action I suggest might cost somewhat more than current general practice, it offers the chance of making the company's investment far more secure. And what is more important, the interests of the United States and the free world would be immeasurably advanced.

Unfortunately there has been a tendency in some quarters to associate social welfare projects and cooperatives with the extension of socialism, perhaps because at the present time the only instruments available to carry out such programs are governments. But by encouraging private and voluntary associations such as trade unions to take up social welfare causes, we would in fact be defending and extending the free economic and social order. By giving status and economic strength to trade unions and similar organizations in the less-developed countries, we encourage their independence, promote their freedom, and enable them to assert further their traditional function of defending the best interests of workers. Even though many of these groups may now be in fact creatures of their governments, we can assist them in developing the integrity of purpose and function which can lead to self-support.

American managers who doubt the efficacy of encouraging trade-union development might well consider the example of the International Petroleum Company, Limited, which has been operating in Peru since the 1880s. In recent years there has been a good deal of popular agitation to nationalize the company. This reached a head in the fall of 1960 when the Peruvian Congress had a nationalization bill before it. There seemed little doubt that it would be passed, and International Petroleum expected to be out of business within the year. But the company had a long and well-established policy of collective bargaining and had encouraged the growth of a strong, responsible trade union in its operations. To be sure, this had cost money; wages were higher and conditions better than they might otherwise have been. The payoff came, however, when five hundred workers rented a fleet of old busses, collected what cars they had, and drove six hundred miles over the desert, carrying gasoline and water with them. At Lima they were met by another six hundred workers from nearby plants of the company. They paraded through the streets of the capital with banners and placards opposing nationalization. They filled the galleries of the Congress and hooted when pro-nationalization speakers took the floor. Their demonstrations were successful and the company is still in business.

American Business and the U.S. Government

American managers operating overseas do not appear to be as well organized as they should be to deal effectively with the difficult problems of their labor relations abroad.

While there are a number of separate councils and associations of international business, they lack the unity and vigor required to be of real assistance to our businessmen. A lot could be gained by more effective exchange of information. I was struck by this when talking to some managers in Latin America who were complaining that they had tried unsuccessfully to incorporate profit-sharing plans in their collective bargaining agreements. It would have been helpful to them if they had known the profit-sharing experience of many companies doing business in Asia. There it was found that workers coming to large companies from rural areas generally had one thought in mind—to make a small pile of cash and return to their village where they could buy some land and establish themselves as relatively wealthy men. They had no interest in any plan which depended on a long period of employment with the company. This same pattern is not unusual in many developing countries where the vast bulk of the population comes from rural areas and regards land ownership as the only really worthwhile form of wealth.

American companies could also benefit from closer contact with the U.S. government. The government not only collects and assembles quantities of information on the economic and social conditions in every country of the world, but it is capable of giving up-to-the-minute advice on political developments which frequently are of central importance to American foreign enterprise. Moreover, there is an intimate link between foreign policy and the operations of U.S. companies abroad. While the Departments of State, Commerce, and Labor have a variety of formal and informal relationships with U.S. international management, these are in an extremely primitive stage and do not begin to meet the need. As a rule, the government takes little interest in American private enterprise abroad until a critical situation has developed and then it is often too late. In too many cases in the past an ambassador abroad has been reluctant to speak out forcefully about the harm that he may feel an American company is doing in the country in which he is serving. With a few outstanding exceptions most ambassadors have felt that private enterprise is private and, regardless of its effects on our national interest, does not warrant their intervention. This may even lead to inadequate support for a company pursuing a progressive policy that rouses local opposition. Strong political forces at home are sometimes mobilized against an ambassador whose stand becomes too controversial. Furthermore, he has few tools with which to insist that a particular company mend its ways so as to promote the national interest.

It appears quite certain that unless there is an improvement in the behavior of some companies abroad, the government will be urged to take a more active role. This would be unfortunate because it would almost certainly tend to discourage American investment abroad at a time when it is urgently needed. It would appear far better for American management itself, working closely with government, to develop the machinery and techniques necessary to ensure that all U.S. companies abroad operate in their own and the nation's enlightened self-interest.

Obstacles in the Path

For the sake of brevity, I have described in somewhat simplified terms some of the problems facing American business abroad and my views of the way in which U.S. companies should approach labor relations. Obviously, not all these observations apply equally to all circumstances; the range of conditions in underdeveloped countries is great. And even when the diagnosis applies, there will often be serious obstacles in the way of carrying out the policies I have proposed.

Generally, those industries which have pursued the most

enlightened practices in the developing world are those which are expanding or enjoying high profits—steel, bauxite, and oil, for example. Problems seem to exist in the older, less profitable industries, such as bananas, sugar, and copper mining. It is easy to be benevolent when you are making a lot of money; more difficult when you are not. It is perhaps the large, plantation-based industries which have the biggest problems. While their difficulties are undoubtedly great, they should remember that Castro's support came from the *campesinos,* that in Brazil the peasant leagues of the northeast are potentially the greatest political force in the country, and that in many countries future revolutions will be increasingly centered around peasants.

Many companies who may want to do the right thing abroad confront a variety of divided loyalties which make it extremely difficult for them. While they may be forward-looking, the government of the country in which they are guests may not be. Furthermore, the U.S. government may or may not be sympathetic with the aims and procedures of the local government. A company's approach to labor problems must be in terms of the local situation. All that can be said in general is that an American company should use what power and influence it has to press responsibly on both the United States and the local government for those reforms and enlightened practices which would satisfy the just aims of the new revolutionary forces abroad in the world, and should guard against preserving an unjust status quo, however pleasant and profitable it may be in the short run.

Then, too, it is not always easy to discern precisely what is good and patriotic. Our government is frequently obscure in setting forth what our policies and objectives in an area or country may be. American embassies too frequently fail to see the forest for the trees, and it is an unusual ambassador who will take the initiative in creating or changing basic policies, especially when such action may be counter to the prevailing wind in Washington. One cannot really put the whole burden of foreign policy fulfillment on business.

In dealing with workers' organizations in a developing country, as I have pointed out, a foreign manager may find himself sitting across the bargaining table from a trade unionist who in a few years will be president or cabinet minister. On the other hand, it is almost as likely that he will be the leader of the opposition. In either case, of course, he will be important to the company's interests, but the political significance of the company's efforts to deal fairly with him or to strengthen his union may be rather different in the two sets of circumstances. At a minimum, though, companies should be aware of this dilemma, which may require better information than some companies now have.

It is all very well to say that some American managers in foreign countries behave badly, do not learn the language, and treat rudely the people in whose country they are guests. As a practical matter, however, companies are limited in their choice of people to send abroad. The number of Americans who are prepared to pull up stakes and go to a faraway, primitive area and run a copper mine, for example—and who are technically qualified—is limited. Perhaps the best recommendation that can be made is that every company should make a special effort to educate and train its personnel serving abroad so that they are prepared as well as possible. This preparation should include well-organized consultation with the appropriate U.S. government agencies. To the best of my knowledge such preparation currently varies widely. Some companies do it well, others not at all. Few if any provide for adequate consultation in Washington. This is as much Washington's fault as it is the companies'.

Whatever is done, a large foreign holding in an underdeveloped country is bound to cause some local resentment and jealousy. One of the great contributions of American private enterprise abroad is that it can demonstrate how to run an efficient, productive operation. In so doing it is extremely difficult for it to avoid unfortunate comparisons with local efforts. To take the lead in social and labor policy, with its inevitable political consequences, can put a company in an exposed position.

Many American companies abroad find themselves saddled with peculiar problems owing to the relatively high wages they pay and the fringe benefits they provide. For example, International Petroleum, which, as we have seen, runs an exemplary operation in Peru, is having difficulties at the Talara oil fields where over the years it has spawned a substantial town. Owing largely to the good conditions and health facilities which the company has provided, the birth rate in Talara has mushroomed and the town has grown a good deal faster than the company. Being isolated, hundreds of miles from the nearest jobs, the young men and women now coming of age in Talara are facing serious unemployment. The company cannot hire them as fast as they come along and there is nowhere else for them to go unless they take the long trek to Lima or some other town or city. Even then it is doubtful that they could find a wage scale as good as International's.

These are quite plainly dilemmas to which there are no easy answers. The best we can hope for is that American business will attack the many problems it confronts in the changing nations of Africa, Asia, and Latin America with the same intelligence, perception, flexibility, and loyalty to the highest principles of our country which has characterized its best contributions to the United States, the world, and mankind.

Chapter VI

THE U.S. GOVERNMENT
AND LABOR ABROAD

Until recently Americans have felt that trade unions in foreign countries were beyond the scope of normal diplomatic relations. Now we have discovered that they are not. The political and economic importance of unions in the newly developing world means that their activities bear directly on the aims of U.S. foreign policy. The fact that in many areas they are the only permanent organizations with any firm roots among the mass of the people gives them an unusual and continuing significance. They are the targets of incessant efforts by international communism for subversion and control.

While the importance of foreign trade unions to the United States is clear, the formulation of policy toward them can be very difficult. In the last two chapters we have seen some of the problems and hard choices faced by American unions and business abroad in their dealings with labor in less-developed countries. The government, too, encounters serious obstacles, some comparable to those of business and labor, others peculiar to the use of public power in foreign territories. Some foreign unions are strong, others are

154

weak. Some are strictly controlled by governments while elsewhere they are independent forces in politics. Even in authoritarian regimes the leaders of controlled unions may have a substantial influence on policies. Frequently unions harbor the opposition and provide the organization for change, good or bad, peaceful or violent, to right or left.

Each of these circumstances poses special problems for U.S. policy. Can we encourage the development of trade unions in a country where they are outlawed? Should we even if we could? Should we aid unions that are under governmental control? Are these decisions to be determined by the current friendliness of the government or by long-run considerations? Can we have an effective policy on these matters without becoming involved in the internal affairs of other countries? How far can we afford to go in becoming involved and how far can we afford to let fear of "intervention" keep us from assisting in the growth of institutions that make for progress and stability?

The place of unions in economic development poses comparable problems. Pressure by unions for higher wages and incomes for their members presents hard decisions to governments that must be concerned with maintaining a high level of domestic savings for development. But unions can themselves undertake various sorts of development activities, directly or through cooperatives. They are often useful in the mobilization and training of a labor force. Because of its involvement in the economic development of many countries, the United States cannot close its eyes to the part unions play in helping or hindering the process.

Judgment about American policy on these matters is complicated by a problem I have pointed out in earlier chapters. Our views about the right and proper role of unions are inevitably shaped by our own history. But the circumstances in underdeveloped countries are different. How far can we reasonably go in urging that the ultimate aim should be an economic and political system that ensures labor freedom from government domination and permits labor and management to deal with one another without undue governmental interference? What alternative arrangements are best suited to the needs of new nations?

Even the apparently clear-cut issue of our opposition to communism presents difficulties in the formulation of American policy. Is it always possible to say precisely what is and what is not a Communist or an anti-Communist trade union? Is an Asian or African leader who looks like a Communist today necessarily going to act like one tomorrow? And if Communists do gain control of an important and strong union in a less-developed country, what should American policy be?

There are probably no general answers to all these questions that will be applicable to all the situations with which our policy must cope, but we cannot afford to throw up our hands and say that we can have no general policy aims because circumstances differ so greatly. So long as we bear in mind the complexities of the problems and the conflicts that will sometimes be inevitable within our policy, we can discuss the main issues more broadly.

Our Aims

The worker organizations of the newly developing world are in many ways the ground swell behind the wave of the future. And this wave is not communism as much as Mr. Khrushchev would like to have us think it is. It is social reform, social revolution if necessary, human equality, individual dignity. It is a house where there has been a mud hut, a hospital bed where there have been death and disease, a school where there has been ignorance. It is justice where there has been oppression, and a fair distribution of wealth where there has been perfumed luxury lying close beside stinking poverty. It is national independence and self-determination. It is the realization of the historic pride which moves all peoples everywhere. This is the wave of the future; it is with this that the United States must become inextricably connected.

Communism has seemed to some to offer a way to achieve these aims. But many who have flirted with communism are learning, some the hard way, that in reality it is more a recurring wave of oppression than of progress. They have learned that a new and dreadful form of oppression breeds in Moscow and Peking. In many countries the worker organizations and their leaders have been the first to learn this awful truth and to sound the alarm.

We should remember that not long ago we were told that Egypt, Syria, Iraq, and the Persian Gulf were gone to the Communists. Quite the reverse has happened. Syria, Iraq, and the Persian Gulf states are not Communist, and President Nasser is still resolutely jailing every Communist he can lay his hands on in spite of the frantic complaints of the Soviets. The editor of the authoritative Cairo periodical, *Al Ahram*, on August 4, 1961, went to great lengths to point out the differences between communism and what he calls "Arab socialism." "Arab socialism regards individual ownership as a right, which must be promoted and expanded . . . the individual is the foundation of the social structure and the state is an apparatus of the people set up to achieve and guarantee justice. . . . Sacrifice, Arab socialism says, should not exceed the limit. . . . We call for work but we refuse conscription." Given the recurring waves of nationalization of private industry by Nasser, it is hard to know how seriously we can take this interpretation of Arab socialism but, at least as theory, it must be an irritant to the doctrinaire Communist. Guinea, which was said to be also gone, appears to be tiring of the invasion of Soviet technicians and is more than likely to emerge as another African neutral, subservient to no one. Furthermore, it appears that all of North Africa will take a more and more strenuous line of independence and nonalignment with any bloc.

And, of course, this is the way we want it. It is our policy to support and assist all nations in their struggle for freedom. But while we can and should advise if we are asked, we must never pretend that we know all the answers to their problems. The newly developing countries must find their own solutions to their own peculiar sets of problems. There may be portions of experience from the United States which will be useful, but given the striking differences in history, circumstances, environment, population, and challenge, it is ridiculous to suppose that our system is transportable intact.

Trade unions are playing an important role in helping many countries solve their problems in a spirit of social justice. In a variety of ways they are keeping afloat the interests of workers. We cannot expect to impose on them our patterns of trade unionism any more than we can expect their governments to adopt intact our economic or political system. In many developing countries today there are authoritarian regimes, and these countries are probably going to require strong central leadership for some time to come. They do not feel themselves ready for our form of democracy. If it were tried, many of them would more than likely go up in the smoke of tribal rivalry, bitter and fanatic internal dissension, and Communist subversion and take-over. In several countries whose continued strength is of the utmost importance to the free world, trade unions are under the firm hand of the central government. If they were not so, it is more than likely that they would either disintegrate or be taken over by fanatical and destructive elements. Surely it is not in our interest to encourage any course of action that would lead to this end.

To be sure, we in the United States feel strongly that trade unions should remain free from domination by the government, the political parties, employers, or church. This is right for us and works best for us. Our trade unions have drawn great strength from this doctrine and they have made great contributions to the American system under it. But it would be wrong to say that because this has been our experience, it is necessarily right for India, Egypt, Ghana, Tunisia, Venezuela, Mexico, and many other countries. INTUC severed from the Congress party in India today would be seriously weakened and would quite probably split apart and dissolve, leaving the Communists an important vacuum to fill. If Nasser tomorrow dropped all governmental controls over trade unions in Egypt, the result in terms of U.S. interests would at least be questionable. Similarly in Tunisia as well as other developing countries it is quite possible that a certain amount of governmental interest if not intervention in trade-union matters is a necessity for the moment. Our view of nations such as these should be governed more by a consideration of practical alternatives than by an absolute standard, taking full account of the trends which appear to be developing and assessing these trends against the requirements of U.S. foreign policy.

The United States is also identifying itself with the widespread movement for social reform. Therefore, we should support the development of strong worker organizations as strong engines for social reform, for the better distribution of existing wealth, for the creation of new wealth, and for the total development of their societies. We should encourage them to find their own best way to solve their own problems. If it happens to coincide with U.S. experience, so much the better. If it does not, as it has not, for example in Israel or Tunisia, our encouragement should not lessen. We should support foreign unions in so far as they are moving honestly and responsibly to improve the lot of their membership and at the same time strengthen the freedom and independence of their country.

The aim of the United Sates is not to have all nations become like us. We are not the Soviet Union. We do not want punch-press copies of our country around the world. We want only to encourage strong, free, independent nations capable of deciding for themselves what they want.

The Range of Policies

The proposition that the United States should support the growth of non-Communist trade unions is nothing new. For some years our government, under both Republican and Democratic administrations, has subscribed to this idea. The problem has been that the government has not gone much beyond accepting the general principle. I say this despite the fact that the executive branch has spent some $13 million a year on international labor affairs.[1] Of course, this figure pales when one considers that Defense Department expenditures total more than $20 million a day.

Too little has been done, and in international labor matters the government has been plagued by policy confusion, a paucity of initiative, insufficient coordination and direction, and a lack of the capacity for flexible, imaginative, and quick reaction to the changing challenges before us. To understand the scope and problems of the government's current operations concerning foreign labor, let us imagine ourselves in receipt of a hypothetical confidential report

[1] This figure includes all of the travel and expenses of foreign labor visitors; salaries, expenses, and clerical support for all labor attachés and labor reporting officers as well as ICA labor officers and State and Labor Department labor officers; U.S. contribution to the ILO; USIA labor budget; labor participation in trade fairs; ICA's manpower development work; and research and publications on labor problems by the State and Labor Departments.

from a competent and outspoken labor attaché in a newly developing country. While very few if any countries will have all the programs going on within them that are described here or will be plagued with all of the problems mentioned, this report will exemplify some of the difficulties.

REPORT FROM DEVELOPING COUNTRY X TO THE DEPARTMENT OF STATE:

This report covers activities by the Embassy and the AID [2] Mission during the past year in the labor area.

1. Three-month courses, financed and run by AID, are given at a local university for trade unionists on the history of the American labor movement, collective bargaining, and union organization and finances. Classes are held five nights a week for three hours a night, and may include as many as 250 students a year. The courses are also extended to others through correspondence and regional seminars.

In general, this educational operation has been a success and it should be expanded, but it has a number of faults. It concentrates too much on American practice and experience, much of which has little application to the local problems and is needlessly confusing. The courses should be directed more at the special and particular needs of labor in the country and should avoid the implication that the best way is our way.

Two of the teachers in this program are Socialists, perhaps Marxists. While this fact undercuts the Communist claim that such courses are an aspect of U.S. "imperialism," and indicates that we are not seeking to impose a slavish copy of our own system, these teachers tend to create an imprecise image of the American economic system, perhaps because they do not fully understand it themselves. They

---

[2] I shall assume for the purposes of this example that AID carries on the same kinds of labor programs as its predecessors did.

have also caused a little stir among Catholic trade unionists who do not understand why we are associating ourselves with such types.

2. The United States Information Service (USIS) publishes a labor paper that goes to about ten thousand persons throughout the country. This has had some success, although it so closely reflects the Embassy's views that it is suspect. A similar problem exists concerning the weekly fifteen-minute USIS labor radio broadcasts.

3. Movies on subjects of general interest are in high demand by labor groups and are lent by USIS when and if they are available. In addition, USIS has four mobile units which tour outlying areas, showing labor as well as other sorts of movies.

It is essential that we be supplied with more motion pictures suitable for union groups. We also badly need an additional mobile unit and operator who can go into rural areas and show movies. There is a great scarcity of films in the local language. We have tried to get all the films available in this continent and from Washington, but still we have only four on labor and they have been shown so often that the audiences are beginning to chant the dialogue from memory, even though they are in English. They are not really that good.

We need new labor films badly and suggest that the American or, perhaps even better, the Canadian labor movements be asked to supply some, stressing the elementary principles of trade unionism, which might be useful down here. Even if we could have magnetic strips for the films we now have, translating the dialogue into the local language, it would be better than nothing.

4. USIS also distributes a substantial quantity of books and pamphlets, some of them in the local language, but in many cases funds are insufficient to allow translations to be made. This makes them useless to most workers.

5. *The Ambassador has made a substantial and successful effort, unlike his predecessor, to include local labor leaders on the Embassy guest list for dinners and receptions. He has offered cocktail parties in their honor and has invited those recently returned from the United States to comment publicly on their trip, whether they are critical or otherwise. He has visited them in their union offices and regularly attends union ceremonies. This has been extremely effective in building friends for the United States within this key element.*

6. *About twenty trade unionists have gone for training in the United States or Puerto Rico. Most of these have come back more friendly to the United States than when they left, but several problems are worth mentioning. Those who went to the United States felt that they spent too much time traveling around seeing sights and visiting trade-union establishments which had almost no meaning for them in their own situation. One said he had wanted most to learn how to run a mimeograph machine so he could put out an anti-Communist newspaper to fight the opposition union. This he didn't learn. Another felt that visiting union headquarters in the big cities was very interesting but didn't help him much. He gave the impression, in fact, of being frustrated and depressed by the vast gap between his situation and that of his U.S. colleague. Others seemed to have learned little more than that being a successful trade-union leader means having a big desk and a pretty secretary in a marble building.*

Those who went to Puerto Rico, on the other hand, felt they had learned a good deal more of practical value to them in their own situation. Here they could see the sort of development taking place that they hoped for in their own country. They could see trade unionists tackling problems that confronted them too. And they were impressed.

7. There is no program which reaches the peasants who are the vast majority of the workers in this country. The Communists are making a concerted drive to organize peasant unions with considerable success. The opposition is weak in the fields and jungles, and it is receiving little assistance or encouragement from the United States. A mobile USIS truck may come through once a month with a movie and some pamphlets. The workers enjoy the movie, although they can't understand it since the sound track is in English; some of the pamphlets they can understand, although most of them are in English too. In any case, the effect is pretty pale beside that of the Communists, who have built a rude hut for a recreation hall, show movies regularly in the native language, and have plenty of glossy brochures, all in the native language and filled with pictures.

8. The International Labor Organization is doing extremely good work with the peasants, seeking to improve their housing, skills, and farming methods. The agency came to ICA a year ago for two bulldozers to build a road, but has heard nothing yet. Washington, it is said, is still considering the matter.

9. Several trade unionists from the United States are working in the country as members of a team sent by an International Trade Secretariat. They are extremely well liked, speak the language, and are doing an effective job; but they are handicapped by lack of funds. They have been particularly successful in helping to build a strong, responsible union of communications workers. This union, which is of great political importance because of its size and organization, is in a close fight with a Communist rival. The government, which is anti-Communist, is doing what it can to be of assistance but its resources are limited. The American trade unionists encouraged the communications workers to appeal to AID for help in starting a self-help worker housing project for their membership. The union asked for two

technical assistance experts, some bags of cement, and $300,000 to get them started. AID here has recommended to Washington approval of such a program, partly because of its enormous political significance in the country, but also because similar self-help housing projects have worked extremely well elsewhere. Washington, however, said that it had never engaged in such a project with a trade union and this would require careful thought. That was six months ago. The communications workers are under increasing Communist pressure, are unable to get wage increases for their membership owing to the government's austerity program, and fear that unless they can provide their members with the housing they desperately need they will be seriously weakened. They are going to appeal to the Inter-American Development Bank for a loan for the project next week. The Embassy strongly recommends approval of such a loan.

10. It would appear important that AID in the future institute a training program in labor-management relations for both trade unionists and management. It is essential that, as the country increases its industrialization, local employers acquire a more enlightened conception of their role in society. They continue to conform to the nineteenth-century mold of the exploitative capitalist and have little conception of their responsibilities. Similarly, labor, including the anti-Communists, sees itself engaged in a class war. Labor and management have little awareness of their mutuality of interest and collective bargaining is extremely difficult for them to understand. We would suggest grants to pay for teams of managers and trade unionists to come together to the United States and Puerto Rico to study labor-management relations. Another possibility would be grants to the local Ministry of Labor to allow it to provide industrial relations training here.

11. The Embassy is badly in need of funds for special projects. We have recently received the following requests *which we have been unable to meet because of lack of funds: prizes for athletic contests among labor groups; a scholarship for the child of a labor leader who was killed recently when he fell down an unprotected mine shaft; shoe machinery to allow a union to start a cooperative to make shoes for the children of workers who now have none; a contribution to a union charity fund. The Embassy believes a small amount of money for these purposes would be extremely useful. Our friends find it hard to understand how we can spend $300,000,000 on military aid and yet cannot meet such simple requests as these.*

12. We had a trade fair here recently and, while it succeeded in selling a good quantity of American goods, it was a failure in other respects. There was an admission charge of sixty cents, about a day's wage in this country, which meant that it was difficult for any worker to attend. The labor team with the fair did extraordinarily well. Its members were American trade unionists who spoke the local language fluently and did a first-class job of explaining the role of labor and trade unions in the United States. But the exhibit accompanying them was small and, although they had five hundred pounds of literature with them, it was all in English and practically useless. The exhibit of "an average American apartment" was unbelievable. No American here had ever seen one like it. It was so modern that the furniture was hardly recognizable as such. No one in this country knew whether we were showing off a gymnasium or a house. The best part of the exhibit was the model University Book Store which had a large and varied collection of books, but again they were all in English, so there was little interest in it. The electrical appliances didn't work because they couldn't be plugged in to the local voltage. The person who drew the biggest crowds was an American baby photographer who just happened to be in town and was hired as a consultant on the spot. He showed people how to take pictures of a baby.

A problem arose over the use of the soda fountain. At lunch time, only the American fair employees were allowed to use the fountain. All others were herded away, obviously discontented.

While this report is fictitious, the programs and problems listed in it are not. I know of no country which has enjoyed or suffered them all at once, but they constitute a fair sample of the good and the bad elements in our foreign operations in so far as they impinge on labor in the developing world. As a government we have accomplished much, but quite obviously it has not been enough. Washington is in general agreement that there is an urgent need for improvement. There is a realization that we need new ideas and the ingenuity to carry them out. This is progress in itself, because it was not long ago that our national leaders had very little conception, if any, of the importance of trade unions in the new society of the world.

Even today there are some in high places who will tell you that all this is very interesting but it is a "peripheral problem" and not of the same order of magnitude as Cuba, Berlin, and Laos. In a sense this is true. There are few headlines in *The New York Times* about labor in the developing world. The great columnists devote little attention to it. It is rarely the subject of dinner conversation among the Washington elite. It is rarely seen as a crisis and therefore gets noncrisis, second-level treatment from the bureaucracy. Few understand that it is, in fact, at the heart of the matter, and that if we are going to avoid a procession of Cuba-Laos situations, we must give first-level, priority attention to the labor factor.

Military assistance, as we have seen, is a horrible waste, and worse, if the people who receive it do not want to shoot in the right direction. Millions for the defense of a developing country will not serve their purpose if the people believe other things are more important. If, for example, within the last five years we had encouraged the growth of strong peasant organizations in Laos and South Viet-Nam, we might quite possibly have built elements into those societies which today would be ready, willing, and able to fight for their freedom. It is worth remembering the key role of the rubber workers in Malaya's fight for freedom from communism.

Why should a man risk his life defending what he doesn't like? It is not a question of communism. We are wrong to make this the issue. In some places the Communists have caught on faster to the central issue than we have. They are encouraging institutions and organizations which will bring about those necessary changes which do not conflict with Soviet aims, and they are working constantly in the fields and jungles to do it. The challenge to us is to do a better job of change in the fields and jungles than the Communists and to show that the required changes can be made and at the same time freedom and individual dignity enhanced. If our ideological intention is merely anti-Communist, we will fail. No one will fight something for nothing, especially when the something appears as attractive as the Communists can make it.

The Communist ideology will eventually take care of itself. It is so riddled with falsehood and invalidity that it is only a matter of time before the developing peoples realize how cruel the hoax really is. But we are fighting subversion as well as an ideology and we must make sure they have the time. They are impatient. They are insisting on change, reform, and if necessary revolution. We must make that change successful and harmonious with freedom and national independence.

Worker organizations are an important vehicle in this effort. They are not on the periphery. They are at the heart of the world. And we cannot afford to let the glare of crisis blind us to their significance. They cannot be relegated to the category of just another nongovernmental organization and left prey to routine bureaucratic handling or, even worse, to no handling at all.

Organizing for Labor Policy

Our past failure to give adequate attention to labor questions in the formulation of foreign policy is reflected in the unsatisfactory division of responsibilities in Washington.

The Department of Labor, with responsibility for domestic labor matters, also has in it the Bureau of International Labor Affairs, headed by an assistant secretary. While the functions and responsibilities of this assistant secretary and his bureau have never been precisely set forth and while his authority has been the subject of vigorous interagency disagreement, it would appear that he has responsibility for the planning and development of broad foreign labor policies and programs for the whole government. He has in his charge the largest and most expert staff in Washington on the subject of labor abroad. This staff collects and analyses a vast amount of international labor information and is in a position to make recommendations based on this analysis with a view to promoting the U.S. national interest abroad. In addition, he has at his disposal the entire resources of the domestic branches of the Department of Labor which can provide him with the latest thinking on technical labor matters, such as collective bargaining, labor-management relations, labor standards, employment service operation, labor department administration, labor laws, and manpower training. Not only does the assistant secretary have the most competent and far-reaching staff in labor matters behind him, but also, by way of the secretary's position in the president's cabinet and his own status as a presidential appointee, he has access to the highest levels of policy formulation. There is at present, however, no machinery through which he can regularly contribute to the formulation of policies and programs on international labor.

Under the Eisenhower administration a start was made to ensure that the labor factor abroad was reflected in the development of foreign policies and programs. The assistant secretary was given representation on all of the working parties of the Operations Coordinating Board. He himself could regularly attend the Planning Board of the National Security Council and he had a permanent seat in the Council on Foreign Economic Policy. Even with this participation in the government's foreign policy councils, however, the assistant secretary lacked the authority to direct and coordinate international labor policy and programs. With the dissolution of the OCB and the CFEP by President Kennedy, even this channel of communication was destroyed. President Kennedy has replaced the previous administration's boards and council by a series of "task forces," concentrating on special areas and assignments. Labor may or may not have representation in these force groups. In any case, there is still no over-all direction or coordination.

Today, therefore, the assistant secretary of labor for international affairs has no formal or regular way of making the unique contribution to policy development which is his to make. This would not be of such importance if there were anyone else in government who assumed this function. But there is not, at least as of this writing.

The Department of State, which has responsibility for the formulation and direction of foreign policy, has a staff of seven men who deal with labor questions: one labor adviser in each of the five geographic regional bureaus, a special assistant to the secretary of state for labor affairs, and his deputy. These men are so busy with crises and brush fires that it is impossible for them to undertake alone the whole task of directing and coordinating policy development and operations in the labor area.

The International Cooperation Administration—predecessor of the Agency for International Development—had an Office of International Labor Affairs with a substantial staff to carry out its assistance programs in the labor area. ICA in theory was under the policy direction of the secretary of state. As a practical matter, however, very little long-range thinking about foreign policy implications went into its labor programs, nor was there much imaginative and creative thought as to how they could be improved. ICA was always quite reluctant to accept suggestions along this line from the assistant secretary of labor for international affairs, the argument being that State and not Labor had authority over it. The transformation of ICA into AID will, hopefully, bring better administration of these matters. There is no longer a central office for handling labor affairs; each geographic bureau handles its own. It is too early to say yet what will be the results of this reorganization.

The Department of Defense, of course, has a vast array of labor problems constantly cropping up on our overseas bases which have extremely serious foreign policy implications. Labor problems at the SAC base at Casablanca, for example, were partly responsible for our being forced to agree to abandon the base. Lack of high-level appreciation of the importance of labor policies and programs has made continuing difficulties for the air force in Okinawa and Korea as well. While the Defense Department has a small staff of labor advisers, it cannot, and does not pretend to, have the Department of Labor's technical knowledge of labor-management relations or international trade-union affairs. And yet there is no formal or even informal arrangement whereby the Defense Department can use the resources of the Labor Department.

The United States Information Agency should have a vast role to play in international labor matters, interpreting American labor to workers abroad, explaining in an understandable way the intricacies of our economic system, and assuring the workers of the developing world that we are on their side. Over the years, however, USIA in Washington has had one man with responsibility for labor, and again there has been only the most primitive arrangement whereby USIA could draw upon the skills and knowledge of the Department of Labor.

There has been and still is, therefore, an extremely haphazard and uncoordinated arrangement in Washington for the handling of international labor affairs. Bureaucratic jealousies in this area have run unusually high and many good ideas have been scuttled because they came from the wrong place and were a threat to someone's empire. There is no perfect answer, but all things being considered, I would urge the following.

While a good argument could be made for making the assistant secretary of labor for international affairs responsible for the direction and coordination of policy and operations concerning international labor, I do not believe it is a realistic possibility. The Department of State is not likely to forgo its primary responsibility in all matters of foreign policy, including international labor policy. The most practical course would seem to be, therefore, to make the special assistant to the secretary of state for labor affairs specifically responsible for the direction and coordination of foreign policy and operations in the labor area. He should be the chairman of a new International Labor Policy Committee with the assistant secretary of labor serving as his vice chairman. This committee should be composed of representatives from the Department of Defense, USIA, and AID. It would make policy and operations plans, using the resources of its member agencies. The Department of Labor would be expected to take the initiative in developing policies and plans for the committee's consideration. Once these plans had been approved they would be put into effect by the appropriate agency operating abroad.

This arrangement would, hopefully, diminish the rivalries presently at play. It would get the most from all concerned and could ensure clear lines of authority and maximum effective application of good ideas. There would not have to be any change in the present functions and responsibilities of the assistant secretary of labor for international affairs and his bureau concerning leadership in U.S. participation in the International Labor Organization, participation in the formulation of trade and tariff policies, direction (under contract with AID and State) of the foreign trade union visitor-training program, and heavy responsibilities in the selection and assignment of labor attachés.

Whatever the bureaucratic arrangements, the main requirement is to ensure that policy concerning labor abroad is effectively made part of our total effort and is not considered a separate matter to be dealt with apart. The political and economic significance of worker organizations in India, for example, should be a vital factor in our policy toward that country, whether it be in relation to economic aid, Food for Peace, information and cultural affairs, or straight diplomacy. For instance, if we are considering assisting the Indian government to build a steel mill we should take into account the important struggle between Communist and non-Communist trade unions in India. Our assistance should be given in such a way as to encourage, so far as we can, the development of a strong, non-Communist trade union at the site.

This means that consideration must be given to a variety of matters not normally considered as part of building a steel mill. Providing workers' housing, hospitals, and schools in the primitive parts of India constitutes a major difficulty.

At Bilhai the Russians built a huge community center for Indians and Russians alike, providing equal service for all. The eyes of many Indians will be sharp enough to see whether we do better than the Russians did in this regard as well as in building the mill. Major installations of this sort offer a great opportunity to provide not only a good production facility but, in some ways more importantly, an example of how Americans work, showing democracy in action. We have an opportunity to encourage the growth of a good workers' organization, to strengthen it by assisting it in providing the services required by its members, perhaps to help it establish clinics, schools, and recreation centers, certainly to teach and practice the best of American industrial relations. We can show how a union, through well-established grievance procedure and collective bargaining, can help its members and provide a stabilizing influence in the community. We can leave behind a framework for continued progress and stable relationships.

To take another, quite different example, labor should have a better place in the international trade fair program. These fairs are not meant to be for the exclusive purpose of selling U.S. products. They are primarily for the purpose of exhibiting and explaining our way of life, our economic system, our productive capacity, our fair distribution of wealth, and the means by which we have achieved a good measure of social justice. In spite of the fact that it is generally agreed that the labor teams at these fairs have done an extraordinarily effective job and generally hold the biggest crowds, labor has been given short shrift in this program. Labor considerations have not been taken into account at the planning stage. Insufficient space and attention are given to labor subjects and thus the fairs fail to portray as effective an image of America as they might.

Our information services abroad should also give much more attention to the needs of labor. They could, for instance, prepare, translate, and make available in large quantity technical materials useful to workers, including extensive do-it-yourself instruction and information on such subjects as nutrition, home economics, accident prevention, gardening, first aid, personal hygiene, and child care. Simple textbooks in mathematics, science, history, and geography would be appreciated in many countries. More USIS material should be put into foreign languages. The distribution of films and literature should give more attention to labor and social problems.

Labor policy should be a vital ingredient in many other kinds of activities as well, such as the Japanese visitor program; Food for Peace in Brazil; Inter-American Development Bank loans in Ecuador; aid to Indonesia, Nigeria, Yugoslavia, or the United Arab Republic; military base policies in North Africa, Okinawa, or the Philippines; the Voice of America; the Peace Corps. We can no longer afford a system of government organization in which the labor aspects of economic, military, and political activities are fringe considerations, taken into account only if some enthusiastic individual happens to bring them to the attention of a high official at a cocktail party or has the fleetness of foot to make an end-run around the system and get these problems considered in the higher councils of Washington.

Devising a Policy

The general principles that should guide U.S. policy on international labor matters are clear enough:

1. We cannot be content merely to be anti-Communist. Our concern is not to line up the nations of the world and label those which are pro-Communist or anti-Communist. We are trying to strengthen national independence, encourage the dignity of the individual, and promote social justice in an environment in which the state is the servant of

man and not the other way around. It is because communism linked to Soviet power is unalterably opposed to these things that we regard it as an enemy.

2. We should seek to ensure that workers have the means and opportunities to receive their full share of the benefits flowing from economic and social development.

3. We should make clear that the United States has equal respect for working people and for employers; that we are dedicated to increasing the educational opportunities of working people, especially their children; and that we are urgently seeking to help them become first-class citizens with an opportunity to own their homes and break out of the feudal bondage under which so many now suffer.

4. We should to this end clarify for ourselves and others the economic system of the United States, explaining forthrightly that it is not a "capitalist" system, as capitalism is generally known and described, but is in fact nearer to what most of the developing people in the world mean by socialism—an economy in which the government regularly intervenes in the interest of social justice and the "public consensus." (See Chapter VII.)

By what means should we pursue this kind of a policy? Some of the answers have been implied by what was said in the last two chapters about American labor and business abroad, but there are also matters that are the special province of government.

The United States must be prepared to accept the fact that trade-union practices in the developing world are radically different from our own; that in many countries unions are subject to more control from governments and political parties than we would like for ourselves, but that they are invariably a force moving in the direction of independence, social justice, and reform and that whatever we may think of them they are of increasing political and economic importance. We should, therefore, support the development of trade unions and do all to strengthen them against sub-version by external forces, and to encourage their growth into strong, free, democratic organizations, effectively dedicated to the welfare of workers.

We should encourage, through training and other programs, the development of sound collective-bargaining practices. The government should especially seek to ensure that American management abroad sets a good example and applies to labor-management relations the philosophy and practice which have brought such stability and success to our own system.

We cannot expect unions in many developing countries to maintain their strength and the loyalty of their membership if they limit their activities to the traditional ones of bargaining and negotiation with employers. In most countries the requirements for national saving and the prevailing poverty are so great that a union cannot hope to sustain itself against the hypocritical claims and offers of the Communists if it relies solely on getting higher wages and improved working and living conditions for its members through collective bargaining. While nothing should be done to discourage the collective-bargaining role of trade unions, within the limits of the economic development needs of their nations, non-Communist groups need assistance and guidance in dealing with their immediate situation. They need a reason for being. The problem is how to help them develop the additional and immediate economic tools to serve and hold the loyalty of their membership and to resist through their own efforts the Communist offensive.

At present, U.S. foreign labor policy does not deal with this problem in an effective manner. A good deal of our program is directed at indoctrinating trade unionists with what we conceive to be our political and economic philosophy. Much of it has the character of propaganda and much of it has no meaning, given the problems faced in developing countries. Our attempts to create good will and approval for our system are frequently of no practical help to the trade-union leader of Africa, Asia, or Latin America. He may like us, but that doesn't help him in the desperate battle in which he is engaged. And all too often our message abroad sounds like a defense of the status quo he is trying to upset or modify.

The United States should, therefore, show greater recognition of the social welfare problems confronting labor in the newly developing world. Furthermore it should assist worker organizations themselves to become agents of development for the benefit of their membership. We should assist responsible, democratic trade unions to engage in cooperative enterprises and to provide their membership directly with many of the facilities and services they so desperately need. We should encourage them to engage in self-help housing projects, in the construction and operation of hospitals and clinics, and in the development of a variety of forms of cooperatives to supply workers at low cost with food, clothes, transportation, and the like. We should help them to start credit unions and savings and loan associations and to set up pension and welfare funds.

This approach on the part of unions has worked in Tunisia and Israel, and in some cases in Indonesia, India, and Lebanon, as we have seen. Labor organizations there have grown strong and capable of resisting subversion or overthrow. Their members have benefited. Furthermore the benefits have not come at the expense of any other segment of the society. The union has not siphoned off funds needed for economic development. It has instead used its organization and structure to contribute to general social development. It has done for its members things which otherwise government would have had to do. To be sure, sometimes it has had the help of government, but it has encouraged saving among its people and it has shown them the meaning and responsibility of owning property. It has built itself into a significant entity, which perhaps in some cases is still dependent on the government or a political party, but which has far greater ability to sustain itself than it did before.

By encouraging trade unions to take up economic action projects of this sort the United States would be helping them to become one day the independent forces we would like them to be. We would be contributing to the establishment of a free economic and social order by preparing them to take on their traditional role in the labor-management relationship when industrialization and the general level of wealth proceed far enough to allow it.

One way of helping unions to take on these functions is to aid directly through AID or some other government agency. We saw what a few shoe machines helped to do in Indonesia. This success and the similar experience with a clinic in Lebanon should be sufficient to inspire AID to explore as a regular and routine matter the possibility of extending similar help to trade unions in other developing countries. We could certainly do more of the same in Lebanon and Indonesia. Assistance to Tunisian labor might take the form of training trade unionists in bookkeeping, administration, shoemaking, tailoring, or any of the many trades and skills on which a cooperative depends. One can easily think of other possibilities: a union self-help worker housing scheme for India's new steel industry, a union-sponsored credit union in Tanganyika, a cooperative training center for trade unionists in Nigeria, a union hospital in Ecuador, and so on.

Opponents of this idea argue that governments in newly developing countries want to distribute money for social welfare projects themselves. They want to get the credit for the housing development, the hospitals, or whatever. This is true in some cases. But more and more these governments are realizing that their continued success and stability depend on their encouraging and strengthening non-Communist worker organizations. They are recognizing that it would be very much in their self-interest to provide social benefits in such a way as not only to help the people but also to strengthen a trade union which would then become an institution for stability and growth in the community.

Also it should be remembered that these schemes do not involve large quantities of money. Once the pump is primed, the cooperative tends to flourish on its own. Some bags of cement and a little technical assistance at the start can produce wonders in a comparatively short time. In these enterprises the workers áre working for themselves and for their families. This provides an enthusiasm which is hard to equal.

Opponents also argue that many unions could not afford politically to accept aid from the U.S. government. It would make them appear to be agents of the United States which in neutral areas is sometimes inadvisable. This is a danger, although, in view of the substantial outlays coming from Moscow, too much fear about it may be a little artificial. There are ways to diminish if not eliminate the difficulty. In the first place, most U.S. aid goes to governments for agreed uses. This means that a trade union would be getting money from its own government, not directly from the United States, for these cooperative practices. In a country where there may be Communist as well as non-Communist worker organizations, however, it might be difficult for the government to give to one and not to the other, even if it wanted to. There is, therefore, a good deal to be said for extending aid to foreign unions through the American labor movement and the International Trade Secretariats.

There are various combinations and techniques that could be used. An ITS could go to its affiliated trade union in Ecuador, for example, and encourage it to apply to the national Ministry of Labor for help in starting a housing cooperative. This could be done in the knowledge that AID would be prepared to help with the project if the Ecuadorian government asked it to. The ITS could help the union draft its plans and specifications and assist in the administration of the project until it got well started. A similar route could be followed with the Inter-American Development Bank, which, under its trust agreement, is authorized to make loans directly to trade unions for cooperative and social development projects. Working in conjunction with an ITS in the field this could be a very practical and valuable technique.

Another possibility is for the American labor movement, under contract with AID, to arrange for help to a worker organization in a developing country through an ITS. Assume, for example, that the plantation workers' Secretariat is interested in building strong peasant organizations in the poverty-stricken northeastern section of Brazil where Francisco Julião is making considerable headway with his vigorous anti-U.S. line. Presumably one of the first steps would be to help the peasants in that area build the houses which they so desperately need. Bags of cement and appropriate instruction booklets could be made available through the plantation workers' Secretariat which would assist in the construction enterprise and go on from there to organize the peasants into an effective and responsible organization. A further alternative would be to encourage assistance to trade unions along these lines through the International Labor Organization, which already has done some important and useful work in training for the establishment of cooperatives of various sorts in Asia and elsewhere.

This by no means exhausts the ways in which U.S. assistance could be made available for helping a worker organization to enter into the social and economic development of its country for the benefit of itself and its members. This is the kind of thinking, however, that needs to enlighten our aid effort to make sure that it is successful not only in reaching the people but also in building a more or less permanent institution which will remain, long after the aid is gone and forgotten, to promote the interests of freedom and social justice.

Not all aid need be American. Though there are some obvious drawbacks and difficulties, we should consider what can be done to encourage and perhaps help other countries to aid in the development of strong worker organizations around the world. Israel comes to mind immediately. Histadrut is widely known as one of the most powerful worker organizations in the world. Its remarkable achievements for its members and for the nation as a whole have attracted considerable interest and admiration throughout the developing world. Histadrut leaders and technicians are acceptable in many quarters where an American would not be. They are firmly committed to free world aims. Their experience and patterns of development have already had a profound impact in many countries of Asia and Africa. There would appear to be no reason why the Histadrut example could not be useful for trade unions in some parts of Latin America also. Tunisia also has shown how a strong trade union can contribute to the total development of a democratic nation as well as to its membership. Tunisian labor could be extremely useful in helping its brothers in Africa and the Near East especially, and might be encouraged to do so.

In some countries where communism has already achieved a substantial foothold and where U.S. aid and personnel may be unwelcome or suspect, it might be in our interest to encourage aid from Yugoslavia. It is important to remember that there are few people in the world who have a stronger emotional antipathy to the Soviet Union and Communist China than the Yugoslavs. To be sure, theirs is a Communist regime, but it has been U.S. policy for a long time to invest large quantities of funds to protect the independence of Yugoslavia and allow it to develop its own governmental and economic system in its own way. And

Yugoslavia is changing fast. I heard the Deputy Minister of Labor of Yugoslavia tell the International Labor Conference in June 1961, for example, that his country had become aware of the danger that might result "if the management of the economic and other branches of society remained within the exclusive power of a centralized State." He went on to explain the Yugoslav system of "workers management," which, as a theory at least, may be tending toward democracy, and is certainly of great interest to some new countries. It would be interesting indeed to see Yugoslav worker leaders in Guinea, helping to develop their workers' council system of management under the noses of Soviet technicians, whose government abhors it. This may be entirely unrealistic, but one has to consider alternatives today from the point of view of United States interests; if we have to choose between the two, Yugoslav influence is substantially more desirable than Soviet, if for no other reason than that Yugoslavia is not an imperialistic power.

Exchange Programs

U.S. government programs for training and exchange of visitors from the trade-union movement have in general been extremely successful in encouraging the growth of non-Communist labor organizations in developing countries. Each year these programs bring some nine hundred trade unionists from abroad for a three, six, or nine months' stay in the United States, and permit American union leaders to go abroad to meet and talk with their brothers around the world. In this way an African union leader can see the progress that American unions and our country in general are making in eradicating discrimination; an Indonesian rubber worker can learn the basic methods and techniques of collective bargaining, union organization, and industrial relations; a Venezuelan oil worker can see with his own eyes that the Communist representation of America as a land run by and for the exclusive benefit of the rich is inaccurate. The leaders and members of foreign worker organizations can see at firsthand the extent to which American labor has confounded the one-hundred-year-old prediction of Karl Marx. Also they can correct in their own minds, at least, the erroneous and damaging image of America which is spread abroad by so many of our movies, magazines, and advertisements. They can learn that all our kitchens are not automatic; that every housewife is not a model; that the American family does not measure its success by the kind of car in its garage; that everybody in Chicago is not a gangster; and that all New Yorkers are not neurotic. Likewise, representatives of the AFL-CIO, the United Steelworkers, the Oil Workers, and other American unions can understand better the problems of labor in the less-developed lands, can learn from them and, hopefully, can help them in their quest for development.

But the outspoken report of the observant labor attaché cited earlier made it clear that there are problems to be faced and improvements to be made. It does no good to bring an Indonesian, a Ghanaian, or a Brazilian to the United States, show him around Washington, New York, Detroit, and San Francisco, whisk him through some steel plants and automobile factories and sit him down for routine conversations with trade unionists who have little understanding of or interest in his problems. With such a dose of America it is not surprising that some have returned home more confused than enlightened, painfully conscious of the vast differences between their own country and the United States, having learned little of practical value. On the other hand a visitor whose program is well planned to meet his specific needs, as is usually the case, and adjusted to provide him with the sort of experience that will be useful to him when he goes home, is greatly helped and returns a greater asset to his country. If care is taken to ensure that he has an opportunity for fruitful conversation with an American trade unionist who understands his country and problems and who has an interest in him as a person, a great deal of good can be done for the United States as well as the visitor.

With a program as large as this one, which has been going now since the end of World War II, there are bound to be difficulties and breakdowns. There is bound to be a tendency to send visitors on a stereotyped tour, visiting the same plants, seeing the same people, regardless of what country they come from or what their needs may be. Any long-term effort such as this runs the risk of developing routines which are bothersome to all concerned. There are several ways to keep errors to a minimum and increase the value of these programs.

The governmental agencies involved should continue their efforts to adjust the program of each visiting team to meet its specific needs. The present practice of sitting down with the members of a team at the beginning of their tour and asking what they would like to do and see is all right as far as it goes. It has the advantage of exhibiting the freedom of our society, showing that we have nothing to hide. They can visit Little Rock, as many want to do, Montgomery, Alabama, Niagara Falls, or wherever. The difficulty is that many visiting teams do not know enough about the United States to have an intelligent view about what kind of program would actually benefit them most. We must know more about the visitors, their needs and interests, and do more planning, so that we can suggest to them a course of training and field trips which they will appreciate—perhaps not at the beginning, but at the end of their visit.

Initially most foreign trade-union visitors were Europeans. Today almost all who come on the government program are from the developing world. Their needs are quite different from those of their predecessors. I was struck by this several years ago when we were planning a program for a Ghanaian group. Having in mind the special problems of their country, we concluded that it would be especially useful for the Ghanaian trade unionists to see the American system of farming cooperatives. When they arrived, they were somewhat indifferent to the idea, not having any special desire to spend several weeks roaming the rural Midwest. When they were through, however, they were unanimous in their enthusiasm and felt they had learned something important and useful.

More of this kind of tailor-making is needed. To that end we should place more emphasis on institutional training than we do now. A visiting team now may spend one quarter of its time in the United States taking courses in American trade-union practice and studying our way of life. These courses need to be adjusted more to the needs of the less-developed world. Additional workshop training should be included in which foreign trade unionists could learn such basic skills as bookkeeping, union administration, organizing techniques, formation of cooperatives, how to run a mimeograph machine, or how to publish a union newspaper. I would suggest that at least half of a team's program time in the United States should be devoted to practical workshop training, designed to meet its specific needs. It is important also that so far as possible these courses be conducted in the native language of the visitor. The present system of earphones and simultaneous translation is not good enough. Where interpreters are necessary, they should know enough about labor and labor terminology to interpret intelligently. Field trips should be geared to what the visitor has been studying and should serve to demonstrate what he has learned in class. Such a program will require more funds than are now allotted to this effort, but they would be well spent.

Many times in the past, visiting trade-union teams have been poorly selected. A high-ranking trade-union leader, who is desperately needed in his own country and perhaps can ill afford the time necessary to make a trip to the United States, is sent with a group of rank-and-file members who may have a more carefree attitude toward the trip. Problems of prestige, timing, and programing naturally arise, which in some cases have resulted in an angry leader going home prematurely.

In view of the great differences between our society and that of developing countries, more training should be done in developing countries. Our experience in Puerto Rico has been extremely satisfactory in this regard. Consideration should be given to encouraging increased training in Israel at the Afro-Asian Institute, run by Histadrut, which is currently doing an outstanding job. Regional training centers in Africa and Latin America should be established where local instructors could provide workshop training courses of extreme usefulness. This would mean that instruction could be given in the native tongue of the participants and the programs could be of varying lengths to meet the needs of busy trade-union leaders as well as novices.

There should be much more training devoted to laying the basis for sound and enlightened labor-management relations. Teams composed of labor, management, and possibly government officials, should be given basic courses in collective bargaining, industrial relations, grievance machinery, and the other elements of democratic labor relations. Much United States experience in this area has meaning in the developing world.

Consideration should be given to whether it might not be better if the American labor movement, under contract from the government, took charge of the training of union visitors. Under the present arrangement, the visitors' programs in the United States are arranged by the Department of Labor in close consultation and cooperation with the labor movement. It is quite plainly a government effort. It might be better to play down the role of government in the program and emphasize its union-to-union aspect. This might make it more attractive to neutral organizations, which prefer to avoid close ties with the U.S. government but do not feel that same hesitancy about a relationship with the AFL-CIO.

All our foreign visitors' programs, labor or otherwise, are meeting increasingly stiff competition from the Soviet Union and Communist China. More and more of the men and women who come here have gone or will go to the Sino-Soviet bloc where most are given red-carpet treatment, wined and dined, provided with theater and ballet tickets, and put up at the best hotels. No such thing happens here. The normal per diem for a trade-union visitor to the United States is $8. Out of this he must pay for his hotel, food, and expenses—including theater and ballet. Needless to say in most cities it doesn't go far, and he is exposed mostly to the seamier side of American life. There is no need to be extravagant, but to ask visitors who do not know the ropes to live on less than their American counterparts is self-defeating.

Government and American Business Abroad

As has been suggested in the previous chapter, the government should take leadership in developing closer consultation between itself and American management and labor abroad. There is an urgent need for a realization on the part of all three arms of our foreign relations of the interdependence of their interests. Too often American business fails to see the connection between its actions and U.S. foreign policy. It is eager to come to the government for help when it needs it, but is sometimes reluctant to reciprocate. Frequently the American manager in a developing country sees it as his duty to adjust and conform completely to the attitudes and customs of the business and landowning classes as well as the regime in the host country, without taking any responsibility for leadership in the achievement of social justice and reform.

During a pro-Communist regime in a Latin American country, for example, officials of an American company needed and received U.S. embassy assistance and advice. It was extremely useful to them. When the regime fell to a conservative government, the embassy and American labor representatives urged the company, which controls a substantial portion of the national economy, to encourage the growth of a strong, democratic labor organization and to cease what had been regarded as repressive and antilabor activities. The embassy urged the company to take leadership in bringing the social reform which the people urgently needed and which the leftist government and the Communists had promised; in short, to do in freedom what had been offered through tyranny. The company, however, finding itself with a sympathetic regime, refused to take the advice. Today Communist strength is up. Free trade-union influence is down. Freedom itself is threatened. The people are disgusted with the company and Americans in general; many look back with nostalgia on the pro-Communists' promises, even though they were unfulfilled and hypocritically offered.

It would be one thing if in a case such as this the company alone received the blame for such shortsighted and damaging policies. This is not what happens, however. All but the most sophisticated in the developing world believe that American business is in fact an agent of the government. Few would believe that the company in this case was not acting with the full support of the U.S. government and the American people. The failure of most foreigners to understand the almost unique pluralism of American society would not be so serious if important conflicts did not arise between the separate pursuits of American government, business, and labor abroad. Unfortunately these conflicts are of a sort that hurt our national interests, so there is no time to waste in establishing effective machinery to prevent them, or at least keep the damage to a minimum. It is not sufficient to limit consultation to the field. Machinery must also be set up at a high level in Washington so that the top leadership of business, labor, and government can participate. For if headquarters does not understand the problems in detail, it cannot send the right instructions and the field will be without guidance.

An interesting if exceptional example in this regard is the story of a labor attaché in one of our embassies who bitterly complained about the antilabor policies of an American company in the country where he was stationed. The company, he said, was deliberately trying to wreck a non-Communist union to the detriment of U.S. interests. He went so far as to advise the union himself on the best tactics to follow to preserve its strength against the company forces, confident that if the union was destroyed the Communists would fill the vacuum. The company's industrial relations manager complained to the ambassador and asked for the removal of the labor attaché. Not getting satisfaction, he called the assistant secretary of state in charge of the area in Washington. The assistant secretary, after conferring with the ambassador, called the company headquarters in New York and the industrial relations manager—not the labor attaché—was removed.

Such bickering between Americans abroad sounds and is nonsensical. It arises, however, out of the lack of any established planning and consultative procedures in this field. Some of the issues which might be on the agenda of a government, labor, and business board on international labor problems are: relations with worker organizations, Communist and otherwise; the role of American labor in assisting American management abroad; the role of government in assisting both, and vice versa; relations with local business groups and intellectuals; consideration of how American management and labor can hasten the process of social reform; the handling of a variety of technical but highly important political issues such as job security, unemployment insurance, welfare programs, education, training and manpower development efforts; and ways of ameliorating the frustration and despair of transition from rural to urban life which have always accompanied rapid industrialization.

Consultation of this sort, required in the national interest, would also help American business. For example, many companies abroad are confronted with the need to lay off substantial numbers of workers as new, automatic equipment is installed in their operations. This retrenchment is an especially serious economic and political problem today for oil and mining companies in Venezuela and Peru and for General Electric in Brazil. Naturally it has serious implications for U.S. foreign policy. Laying off a relatively highly paid production worker in one of these countries is an extremely serious thing for him, because the chances are he cannot get another comparable job and may be forced to return to his village and scratch out a meager living for the rest of his life or swell the ranks of the discontented unemployed in the big cities. Some companies, however, have done excellent pioneer work in softening the impact of the layoff. Through proper planning, training, and job placement a great deal can be done. It is important that all American companies observe the very best practices in this regard, and it is perfectly conceivable that they could get government help in doing so.

Business and labor might undertake this kind of coordination and consultation themselves. It is only because there are no signs of their doing so that I suggest that government assume the initiative.

Labor and Government Service

Quite obviously a primary requirement for the kinds of policies I have proposed is that the U.S. government should know what is taking place in and around the trade-union movements in the developing world. We must have men abroad with the capacity, understanding, linguistic ability, and instructions to allow them to make contact with the obscure worker leader of today who tomorrow may be a cabinet officer or president. This means that new and continuing emphasis must be placed on the intelligent selection and assignment of labor attachés in our Foreign Service.

The number of labor attachés has increased dramatically in recent years. For example, three years ago we had one in the whole African continent; now we have seven. In all, throughout the world, as of this writing we have forty-three with eight assistants. In addition ten are on duty in Washington, assigned to the Departments of State or Labor. These are still not enough, however. We should have a labor attaché in every country of the world and, perhaps even more important, we should have several assistants in large countries such as India, Brazil, and Mexico, where labor is of such vital importance.

While the detailed tasks of a labor attaché may differ from post to post, a prime requirement in most developing countries is that he should have the ability to make favorable contact with worker organizations and their leaders. For this reason it is, in most cases, extremely useful for a labor attaché to have had practical working experience in or with the American labor movement. While, as we have seen, the worker organizations of the developing world frequently bear little resemblance to our own, there are certain basic elements of similarity, an identification of sympathies, of understanding, and a common language between trade unionists, which become extremely useful. Furthermore, many of the skills acquired in our own labor movement can be helpful abroad, and it is important for a labor attaché to be able to speak confidently and with knowledge about American labor and its role in our economic system.

The American labor movement is generally held in high regard abroad. It is not too much to say, in fact, that no segment of our society is more generally admired by the people of Asia, Africa, and Latin America. One reason for this is that U.S. trade unions have for a long time contributed generously from the dues of their members to their brothers in the democratic world. Another reason, oddly enough, stems from the fact that the United States is known throughout the world as a "capitalist" society. "Capitalism" in the newly developing countries, to Communists and non-Communists alike, is a nasty word carrying with it implications of exploitation, colonialism, discrimination, and the worst of nineteenth-century monopolistic, imperialistic, robber-baron economics. There is little appreciation abroad of the extent to which the democratic process in the United States has compelled private and government actions to secure social justice. And yet there is an awareness that the American worker enjoys a higher standard of living than any workers anywhere. The African, Asian, or Latin American is apt to explain this seeming paradox by assuming that the American labor movement has single-handedly achieved these high standards by wresting unparalleled benefits from "capitalist" hands. Hence in many countries a labor attaché with an American trade-union background possesses credentials which will open many doors closed to others. To make the most of these advantages the government should increase its program of recruiting highly qualified young men from the American labor movement to serve in the Foreign Service as labor attachés. These men must be especially well-equipped linguistically because as a rule worker leaders speak only their native tongue and a labor attaché who depends upon an interpreter is badly crippled.

For these same reasons it would be useful and appropriate for a properly qualified American trade-union leader to be named an ambassador to some newly developing country, especially one in which worker organizations are playing an important political role. While certainly a non-career ambassador should be appointed for his personal qualities without regard to any system of quotas for various professions—businessmen, lawyers, academicians—it seems odd that no U.S. labor leader has ever been appointed an ambassador. Given the long and useful history of American labor activity abroad, there are many who would be qualified.

A labor attaché chosen from the ranks of organized labor must, of course, sever his union loyalties upon entering the Foreign Service and commit himself to the government and its policies. In the past there have been occasions when there has been some doubt on this point. There have been labor attachés whose loyalties to the AFL or the CIO or the individual union from which they came have remained strongly intact and even superseded their governmental commitment. While today there are few, if any, serious differences between American labor's international policies and those of the government, this may not always be the case. Also, it is important that the government maintain strictly its authority in the appointment and assignment of attachés. There have again been instances where strong trade-union pressure has been exerted to secure a particular assignment for a certain individual. This, of course, dulls the integrity of the system and the morale of the labor attaché corps. Consultation with and advice from American labor on labor attachés, their function, and assignment are helpful and necessary, but there should be no doubt about the government's final authority. This serves the interests of labor no less than that of government: it permits the independence necessary for legitimate criticism of government action with which labor disagrees.

In certain countries, a man with a university-labor background might be more useful than a trade unionist. And in others a person with experience in manpower development or the administration of a labor department or some other governmental agency in the labor field might be more suitable. In addition, some of our best labor attachés have come from the ranks of the regular Foreign Service. Recently the State Department in cooperation with the Department of Labor has instituted a special training program to give young Foreign Service officers the background and education necessary to be good labor attachés. But basically it is not so much training or background or past experience that makes a good labor attaché as it is his own breadth of vision, understanding, sympathy, and perception. The right kind of man, or woman for that matter, from wherever he may come can generally win the necessary acceptance and do the job. As we have seen, an important part of a labor attaché's assignment is to assist American management in any way he can. This requires that in addition to having the confidence of labor he must also have that of American companies in his area. They must regard him as someone whom they can trust and who will provide them with objective information and judgment.

It is also important that it be made easier to move up from being a labor attaché to the rank of minister or ambassador. While there have been some outstanding exceptions to the rule, in general once a man becomes a labor attaché he has tended to remain one. It would be far better if after a number of years in labor work an officer could carry that experience into broader political or economic work and on up to positions of highest responsibility. That would be one of the most effective ways of assuring the full consideration of labor issues in the formulation of foreign policy.

Chapter VII

SOME TRUTHS ABOUT OUR
ECONOMIC SYSTEM*

Time is on our side in the cold war in the sense that as each month passes the leaders of the developing world are seeing with increasing clarity the true dimensions and purposes of Communist imperialism. They are seeing what the magician's hands are doing under the pretty silk. They are realizing that however impressive may be the accomplishments of the Soviet system and however tempting the offers of aid, in both there is an involvement with bondage which is abhorrent.

Nevertheless, this is no cause for complacency or great optimism because time is also short. The spreading network of Communist power is alarming and the recognition of its real purposes is fruitless if it comes too late. Time is only on our side if we use it wisely.

As it is important for the world to know the truth about communism, so it is important for it to know the truth about us. Unlike our adversaries we are not trying to hide or dis-

* Note: An earlier version of this chapter appeared as a U.S. government pamphlet, *The Truth About the American Economic System* (Washington: GPO, 1960).

guise the truth, but unfortunately and unwittingly we tend
to do so.

Judging by many of our pronouncements we are confused
about the precise nature of our economic system. We know
that we have developed a pretty good thing here which
has brought us ever increasing levels of widespread prosperity. We are proud of the democratic nature of our system and the opportunity it gives to all to prosper. And yet
when an American abroad comes to explain the arrangements which we have developed to secure this system, he
frequently speaks in highly mythological and often inaccurate terms. He tends to describe this country as he heard
about it in tales from his mother or even his grandmother,
or as he may have studied it in a history book when he was
a child, or as he thinks it ought to be, or as he would like
to have it. It is a rare American who sets out our economic
system as it is. Phrases, slogans, and jargon get in the way,
such as socialism, capitalism, private enterprise, and the
like. Too few Americans seem to understand what these
words mean to different people, or appreciate that they
cannot be used unmodified and unexplained without causing dangerous misunderstanding.

When the Communists refer to socialism, for example,
they mean complete domination and control of all phases
of the economy by the state. On the other hand, when Prime
Minister Nehru speaks of it, he says: "My idea of socialism
is that every individual in the State should have equal opportunity for progress. I do not at all prefer State controlling
everything, because I attach a value to individual freedom." [1] When an Englishman or a Scandinavian or a Japanese or a Brazilian speaks of it, the word takes on a variety
of different meanings. In talking with an American businessman the other day, I found that he described private,

[1] Speech entitled "Our Conception of Socialism"; typewritten copy supplied by Embassy of India, Washington.

nonstatist cooperatives as socialistic, despite the fact that in the developing world they offer one of the few practical routes to private ownership, initiative, and enterprise.

Similarly, when an American speaks of "capitalism," 99 per cent of his listeners in Asia, Africa, or Latin America will get an image that is in no way representative of the economic system of the United States. Too few Americans go beyond the words and phrases to say exactly what we have in the United States. With shock I have listened to apparently intelligent Americans—government officials, businessmen, congressmen, labor leaders, intellectuals of all sorts—describe our system as it may have been in 1840 but certainly has not been since. For example, I have seldom heard them speak of unemployment compensation, social security, minimum wage, or any of the vast panoply of governmental programs, rules, and regulations which are so significant to the system and without which it is completely incomprehensible. Conservatives and liberals alike when they get overseas seem to overlook these things, or to be slightly ashamed of them as being anti-Emersonian if not downright un-American. It is not necessary, after all, to approve of all aspects of our economic system to describe it accurately, completely, and in a balanced fashion. A Barry Goldwater and a Hubert Humphrey should be able without basic disagreement to describe the system as it is, objectively, historically, and accurately. They may differ on whether it is the way it should be, but surely they can be accurate reporters.

While our confusion about our system is enough to hinder seriously its understanding and acceptance abroad, the Communists make the situation worse by spreading a deliberately false picture of it. This is often done cleverly through a combination of lies, half-truths, and innuendos, sprinkled over with their own inimitable vocabulary and false definitions. Their system is "free," "democratic," and

"popular"; ours is "slavish," "exploitative," and "dictatorial."
Their jargon is as puzzling to us as Humpty Dumpty's was
to Alice:

> "When I use a word," Humpty Dumpty said, in a rather
> scornful tone, "it means just what I choose it to mean—neither
> more nor less."
> "The question is," said Alice, "whether you *can* make words
> mean so many different things."
> "The question is," said Humpty Dumpty, "which is to be
> master—that's all."

However unreasonable it may be, Communist propaganda is especially effective with worker leaders who theoretically have the most to gain in Lenin's "paradise." Given
the significance of these leaders in the developing world,
their attitudes toward our economic system as opposed to
the totalitarian competition become extremely important.
We cannot possibly expect them to work with enthusiasm
on behalf of a system which at best is unclear and at worst
comes to them as a distorted reflection of everything they
despise.

While Americans use the word "capitalism" to describe
their economic order, it bears little resemblance to the mo-
nopoly capitalism of the eighteenth and nineteenth centuries
upon which Marx based his theories. Contrary to his predictions, our economic system has in fact proved to be a
spectacularly effective means for the creation and just distribution of wealth. Arising from free business competition
among people enjoying political democracy, the American
way has been and is more revolutionary than the state capitalism practiced today by the followers of Marx and Lenin.
In fact, it renders the Marxian view of capitalism, socialism,
and communism obsolete. Communists today are fighting
a ghost.

Lenin wrote in his *Imperialism:* "It goes without saying
that if capitalism could develop agriculture . . . if it

could raise the standard of living of the masses, who are everywhere still poverty-stricken and under-fed, in spite of the amazing advance in technical knowledge, there could be no talk of superabundance of capital. . . . But if capitalism did these things it would not be capitalism. . . ." These are the things that have been done by American capitalism, the most effective and egalitarian social and economic system the world has yet known. The exploitative capitalism that Lenin had in mind—and perhaps Mr. Khrushchev too when he boasts that he will bury us—has long since died in the United States, if in fact it ever existed. The system we have is still evolving, providing an ever-widening distribution of wealth.

Americans have difficulty communicating their experience to others. As Jacques Maritain has told us:

> You are advancing in the night, bearing torches toward which mankind would be glad to turn; but you leave them enveloped in the fog of a merely experiential approach and mere practical conceptualization, with no universal ideas to communicate. For lack of adequate ideology, your lights cannot be seen.[2]

Our wealth does not dazzle the foreigner with the virtues of America. The people of less-developed countries are not particularly affected by statistics on how many cars are in American garages or television sets in American living rooms or bathrooms in American homes. After all, even dictatorships can be efficient producers of goods. These people see little relationship between our horn of plenty and their immediate problems. The system by which our horn has been filled is simply known to them as capitalism, without qualification. This word arouses almost unanimous animosity because it embodies attitudes and images of Dickensian

[2] Jacques Maritain, *Reflections on America* (New York: Scribner's, 1958), p. 118.

exploitation which were overcome in the United States some years ago.

In many foreign countries a capitalist is thought of as the economic descendant of the feudal lords, or the representative of monopolies, a foreigner who deposits his profits abroad with little regard for social justice or community responsibility. Capitalism is also a word associated with colonialism and exploitative land tenure, with the man who takes everything and gives nothing. To the average worker in most of the developing countries of the world, whose chief economic concern is keeping body and soul together, a capitalist is the curse of the poor, the villain in the Socialist morality play, the local moneylender, the black marketeer. Unfortunately, most entrepreneurs in these countries do little to change the image. Many of them look upon a 40 per cent profit from investments and 60 per cent from the yield of rented land as being a normal annual reward, while wages in these same countries are often below the subsistence level.

There is little understanding abroad of the role the U.S. government plays in protecting the public against abuses of economic power. Consequently, leaders of developing countries often find it difficult to see why the U.S. economic system should not follow the course laid down by Marx, the rich getting richer, the poor, poorer, and the robber baron increasingly rapacious.

Not knowing that there is an alternative, leaders of less-developed countries have often turned to what they call socialism not so much to place the means of production in the hands of government as to assure that productive facilities will be used with some measure of social justice. What the United States has made out of its free, largely competitive system often approximates in social justice what these people are looking for in socialism. It is certainly not what they associate with capitalism.

In almost all countries seeking rapid industrialization there is a fear of the monopolistic tendencies of traditional capitalism. In these regions with their weak economies and great need to raise the standard of living, talk of the danger of Western monopolies, cartels, and exploitation makes a strong appeal. The profit motive in capitalism is resented as unjust and feared as inflationary and wasteful. Leaders of less-developed countries generally feel the need to impose stringent controls over capital which is badly needed for economic development. Often they see capitalism as another force to fight in conserving this wealth. They do not realize that we, too, in America, while maintaining a free competitive system, have strict controls over our economy.

However desirable it might be, it is probably impossible to disengage ourselves from the word "capitalism," although it is interesting to recall the words of former President Herbert Hoover before he was elected president:

> Like most Americans, I refuse to be damned by anybody's word-classification of [our social system], such as "capitalism," "plutocracy," "proletariat" or "middle class," or any other, or to any kind of compartment that is based on the assumption of some group dominating somebody else.
> The social force in which I am interested is far higher and far more precious a thing than all these.[3]

Be that as it may, words and phrases such as economic democracy, economic humanism, dynamic capitalism, people's capitalism, social capitalism, and American service capitalism may have their uses with various audiences but fall short of fully describing our ways.

In whatever efforts we make to explain our economic system to others, we should clearly recognize that our accomplishments have taken place under extraordinarily fav-

[3] Herbert Hoover, *American Individualism* (New York: Doubleday, 1922), p. 12.

orable conditions. Great quantities of valuable and widely diversified natural resources lie within our national boundaries. We have never been subject to the terrific strains of overpopulation. Generally we have always had enough to eat. But many other nations, too, have had an abundance of resources and yet failed to realize the potential of this wealth in terms of raising the living standard of their people. Our greatest strength may well be the fact that we never had to suffer the feudal system; that through political democracy achieved early in our national history and through universal suffrage we have been able to control the growth of our economy in the interests of all of our people.

It is not realistic to suppose that other countries, particularly those of Asia, Africa, and Latin America, could or would want to adopt our system as it is. Through a proper understanding of our economic order, however, the peoples of foreign countries may know and understand us better and may possibly find portions of our experience helpful to them in solving some of their own problems.

The American system is evolving fast. There has been no time to articulate for it a proper philosophical base in classical form. Its essential characteristic is efficient, competitive production causing economic progress linked with social justice and assured by democratic means. It is a creature of our political system—pragmatic, responsive to the will of the people, and subject to countless checks and balances imposed internally by labor, management, and competition, and externally by government. In contrast to Marxian socialism, communism, or exploitative capitalism, economic decisions in our system are the sum of countless individual decisions rather than edicts handed down either by a handful of robber barons or by the state. The public consensus is the final arbiter of power in the American economy. If the public consensus is not recognized, government intervenes to assure its recognition. Basic to the success of the American businessman is his own realization that he must serve before he gets.

Laissez-faire capitalism was contained, controlled, and transformed in America by three elements, all of which are revolutionary in character, but none of which ever contemplated destroying the whole system.

The first of these elements was the professionally managed American corporation which replaced individual or family owners, the tycoons, and moguls interested only in building personal fortunes. More than half the output of American factories and mines is today produced by about five hundred corporations. Were these the possession of five hundred families or individuals we would probably be suffering from exploitative capitalism. But they are not. The ownership of the corporations is widely distributed; they are becoming steadily more the possession of the many rather than the few. Our corporations have about 12.5 million direct stockholders; even more important, a large and growing amount of their stock is held by institutions, pension funds, trusts, insurance companies, mutual funds, etc. Probably fifty million Americans receive a share of the profits of the five hundred corporations through participation in these institutions. Thus corporations have become in a very real sense public, rather than private, enterprises, serving a large and growing body of stockholders, offering jobs to millions, as well as supplying an enormous number of consumers. They are public, yet they are not of the state.

The managers of these corporations are not owners; they have been called nonstatist civil servants. The corporate system at present is thus operating to "socialize" or "people-ize" American industry but without the intervention of the political state. In addition, the managers of American industry have come to realize that their success depends on an economically strong work force. The magnitude of American managerial effort is obvious in the size of our gross national product of over $500 billion, but the real effectiveness of our economic democracy is demonstrated by the fact that two-thirds of all output is consumed by the American public in the form of goods and services. Basic to managerial philosophy in America today is what in Henry Ford's time was a revolutionary concept: Production for a mass market, plus high wages, makes mass prosperity.

The attitude of the American manager toward workers is also expressed in the value he places on plant safety, good working conditions, and imaginative personnel relations. It is significant that in 1958 the average injury frequency rate from blast furnaces in steel mills in the United States was 3.7 disabling injuries for every million man-hours, compared with 74.7 in 1910.

The second element altering American capitalism is organized labor, a permanent and powerful feature of our economic system. The American worker has never thought of himself as a member of the oppressed proletariat. Through his union he has become an equal partner in the labor-management relationship and bargains collectively—normally without the intervention of government—to secure a just share of the fruits of his labor. His union also protects the American worker's security in his job and his promotion rights. It enables him to determine jointly with management the conditions under which he works, and it assures prompt and equitable handling of his grievances.

Instead of becoming progressively poorer, the American worker has become progressively richer in a capitalist society. During the past thirty years "real" wages of workers have risen about 4 per cent annually, helping the American worker to achieve the highest living standard of any worker in the world. A coal miner, for example, gets about $25 a day. Family income, adjusted for change in the value of the dollar, has risen 50 per cent in ten years.

The American trade-union movement does not feel the

need to form a political party, nor has it identified itself wholly with a political party. It does get into politics very effectively, however, to defend its interests, dealing more or less impartially with both parties. The following words of George Meany, President of the AFL-CIO are worth remembering:

> Collective bargaining, we have learned, can exist only in the environment of political freedom. Where there is no individual liberty, there is no free trade-union movement either. Every dictator, from left to right, as a first step in the consolidation of power has sought to destroy free trade unions. And so we are dedicated to freedom, not only political but also economic, through a system of private enterprise. We believe in the American profit system. We believe in free competition. The American private-enterprise system, despite some defects, has achieved far greater results for wage earners than any other social system in history.[4]

Perhaps the most important of the three elements is the American government which the "public consensus" has persistently refused to permit to become an expression of "the owning class" as Marx predicted. As a result we live under what many would describe as a mixed economy, which seeks to put a floor below which no one can sink but builds no ceiling to prevent a man from rising.

In the less-developed areas of the world and even in Western Europe there is little awareness that government expenditures for various social insurance programs in the United States are around $12.5 billion annually; that another $25 billion or more is expended each year by federal, state, and local governments under various other social welfare programs, such as public welfare, public health and medical care, child welfare, aid to veterans, public housing and education; that, in addition, contributions to private

[4] George Meany, "What Labor Means by 'More,'" *Fortune,* March 1955, p. 92.

health and welfare funds are currently being made at a rate of $8 billion a year; and that the total of $46 billion amounts to roughly a tenth of the current gross national product.

Few Asians and Africans have any idea that the United States has an elaborate unemployment compensation system and few realize the extent of our agricultural programs and federal power establishments. It has been estimated that in the United States about 20 per cent of the gross national product is disposed of by the various levels of government; in India the figure is only 10 per cent. Such statistics point to the difficulty of using the words "capitalism" and "socialism" with respect to the United States and countries like India today.

In our country, all corporations except the smallest pay 52 per cent of their profit to the Federal government, in addition to many other taxes. We have a steeply graduated personal income tax which at the upper levels rises above 80 per cent. Eleven per cent of the American taxpayers—that is, those earning over $8,000 a year—pay 51 per cent of the personal income taxes.

The government regularly invades what might be regarded as the normal sphere of private enterprise to do what the latter cannot do or do so well, whether it be to set up a Tennessee Valley Authority, provide electric service to rural communities, or advise, regulate, and assist the farmer. It is important to note that this sort of governmental activity is not a matter of doctrine or ideology. It is rather the pragmatic voice of the people speaking through the state to get some particular thing done that needs doing.

In the last century when free competition was threatened by abuses, concentrating too much power in the hands of a few to the detriment of the many, Congress passed the Sherman Anti-Trust Act, curbing monopolies and establishing the principle in law that everyone has a right to become a capitalist, but not at the expense of general welfare.

When unscrupulous businessmen sought to palm off on the public dangerous medicine and adulterated foods, Congress passed the Pure Food and Drug Act of 1906, regulating producers. Times have changed since then, and today the majority of goods and services are guaranteed to satisfy the customer; the trade-mark has become a valued and trusted mark of confidence. Some stores even will refund the money for a roast if the housewife doesn't find it tender!

There is a long list of other federal and state regulatory legislation which today has become an accepted and integral part of our economic system, protecting the individual against abuse by banks, insurance companies, corporations, lending agencies, and most recently labor unions. For instance, there was a day when many an innocent investor was fleeced through shady practices with stocks and bonds. Today, however, individuals who violate the provisions of the Securities Exchange Act, for instance by failure to give adequate information about a company whose securities are to be issued or by taking advantage of inside knowledge or manipulating markets, are subject to civil suit and criminal penalties.

Abuse of power by the railroads at the turn of the century led President Theodore Roosevelt in 1903 to ask Congress to empower the Interstate Commerce Commission to fix railroad rates. Today the government regulates the price of practically all forms of public transportation. The failure of commercial utility companies to satisfy the widespread demands for rural electrification led Congress to give authority to the Rural Electrification Administration to encourage the development of cooperatives in this field, many of which have become substantial private enterprises.

It is useful to note the words of Adolf Berle:

No element of the current American industrial system is removed from contact with and dependence on other parts of that system. The relationship with and interdependence of each organization on other organizations is frequently direct and immediate, limiting its capacity to act. In contemporary United States, the power of any organization, however great and strong, is subject not only to the laws of its being but to the added limitation that failure or refusal by it to function means that some other organization—whether a competing organization or an agency of the State—will emerge, undertaking to produce, employ, supply, or distribute, that is, to provide a tolerable equivalent.[5]

While there is, to be sure, great concentration of power in the great corporations of America, the role of small business should not be underestimated. Despite the giant corporations, there is room and need for the small family enterprises similar to those which exist throughout the world. Of all the retail establishments in the United States over 40 per cent are run by the proprietor, with no paid employees. Over another third have three or fewer employees. Together their sales volume is over one-fourth of all retail sales, including those of the large retail chain stores.

There are more than 140,000 manufacturing enterprises in the United States—more than 40 per cent of all manufacturers—with fewer than four workers. Some 300,000, or over 90 per cent of all manufacturers, employ fewer than fifty.

Not all American enterprise takes typical and traditional forms. Raymond W. Miller writes:

> The nonprofit cooperative enterprise is a fundamental part of the American business scene, recognized and respected throughout the nation. To quote the National Association of Manufacturers:
>
>> A "cooperative" is a form of business enterprise that enables a group of individuals, partnerships, or corporations, to combine together for the purpose of producing or buying or selling a commodity or service.

[5] *Power Without Property* (New York: Harcourt, 1959), p. 88.

City consumers have gotten together to buy goods and sell them. Businessmen have formed mutual fire insurance companies. Individuals join together to buy life insurance through a mutual insurance company or merchandise through a mutual wholesale purchasing association. People who save money put their funds in a mutual savings bank. Farmers join together to buy goods they use in production or to sell the things they grow. All of these are "cooperatives." They are also legitimate forms of private enterprise.

One of the fields in North America in which cooperatives are most active is agriculture. . . . Several million American families living in small towns and rural communities secure their electric service through private cooperatively owned power companies (R.E.A.), whose original capital was borrowed from the government, and which is being repaid ahead of schedule. Every bank clearing-house, rural telephone and electric cooperative, mutual building and loan association, mutual insurance company, mutual savings bank, credit union, and cooperative apartment is a sign post pointing to the fact that people in a free society demand and have achieved freedom to organize for their own best economic interests.[6]

The American economic system is not perfect and we know it never will be. We *do not* believe in utopias. We do believe in improvement and progress. We *do* think that the American economic system is the best system for us. We also believe that it shows one of the roads toward the optimum material condition of man: economic power used for reasonable profit and social justice for all with the government as referee and umpire, with freedom and initiative encouraged as business tries to serve as well as prosper.

Of special importance to those countries undergoing rapid development is the flexible quality of the American economic system, its lack of rigid doctrine. To those who are as uncertain about their problems as they are about the answers to them, the pragmatism of the American approach

[6] Raymond W. Miller, *Can Capitalism Compete?* (New York: Ronald Press, 1959), pp. 48-49. Miller's quotation came from National Association of Manufacturers, *NAM and Cooperatives* (privately published in New York, 1946), p. 7.

should have a substantial appeal. It is this in our system that we should emphasize—not the doctrinal aspect which in many cases is more mythological than real. Our only real insistence is upon democracy. Beyond that, what is most effective in a particular place at a particular time to meet a particular need should meet with our approval. If these things are understood the leaders of the developing world should be able to see more easily that for all the differences, our experience may have some relevance for them and above all to understand that there is no need for them to choose between communism and what they—and others—imagine capitalism to be.

Chapter VIII

THE UNITED STATES
AND THE INTERNATIONAL
LABOR ORGANIZATION

The vital importance of worker organizations in the development of the nations of Africa, Asia, and Latin America gives a new and urgent importance to the International Labor Organization. The ILO is the one specialized agency of the United Nations where worker leaders from one hundred nations can sit together with equal rights alongside representatives of governments and employers. As these leaders take on increasing influence and power, this organization takes on new importance as a political forum in which they are exposed to the crosscurrents of the world and have a unique opportunity to put their views before an important international audience.

Few initials have caused more consistent confusion in the United States than ILO. The organization has been misunderstood and misconstrued by many ever since the United States joined it in 1934. Some think of the ILO as an organization of trade unions, others as a world parliament, and still others as a "leftist" operation with dark and dangerous objectives. It is none of these.

It is an eminently practical, specialized agency of the United Nations strongly committed to democratic ideals and posing no threat to any nation's sovereignty. Surprisingly unpublicized in this country, though it is forty-three years old, the ILO has accomplished some of the most remarkable feats of international diplomacy in recent years. In addition, it is bringing help and hope to many millions of people throughout the vitally important less-developed areas of Asia, Africa, and Latin America; and it has done so effectively and economically.

Pope John XXIII, in *Mater et Magistra,* his profound encyclical on social problems in the modern world of May 1961, wrote:

> We are . . . happy to express heartfelt appreciation to the International Labor Organization, which for decades has been making its effective and precious contribution to the establishment in the world of an economic and social order marked by justice and humanity, where also the lawful demands of the workers are given expression.

The Principles of the ILO

Created in 1919 at the Versailles Peace Conference as part of the League of Nations, the ILO brings together employer, worker, and government representatives from one hundred nations in an effort to improve the welfare of workers throughout the world and to assist in the development of those institutions which will ensure the free and just development of societies.

Operating on a current budget of slightly more than $10 million, the ILO holds an annual conference each June in Geneva where its permanent office is located. It has a governing body, composed of twenty governments, ten employers, and ten workers, which supervises the International Labor Office—the permanent staff of the organization—determines conference agenda, and formulates the budget on the basis of recommendations made to it by the director-general of the organization.

Delegations to ILO annual conferences are made up of one employer representative, who in the United States is normally nominated jointly by the National Association of Manufacturers and the Chamber of Commerce; one worker delegate, nominated by the AFL-CIO; and two government delegates, one from the Department of Labor and one from the Department of State. The conference is attended by well over one thousand delegates, advisers, and observers.

Subjects with which the ILO deals are numerous: employment, improved living standards, equal opportunity, sound labor-management practices, the development of skills, protection for the life and health of workers, child welfare, social security, and a number of others.

The ILO is of very special importance to the United States and to the free world as the only organization created to deal with those problems which are most real to the majority of people in the world: work, wages, security, and the right to freedom and dignity. Even though American objections to the League of Nations prevented our joining the ILO until 1934, fifteen years after it was founded, this country has always played an important role with respect to the organization. Its first meeting was in Washington in 1919 and among its moving figures was Samuel Gompers, first president of the American Federation of Labor.

It was no accident that the ILO was founded when it was. The founders, in addition to reflecting the sharp increase in the social conscience of governments following World War I, felt an urgent need to create an international organization which would refute the Marxist theory of the inevitability of class warfare. At the very moment that

Title XIII of the Treaty of Versailles was being drafted to include an International Labor Organization, the French Premier Clemenceau had thirty thousand troops mobilized in Paris to put down a general strike. Defeated Germany was in despair, hopelessly viewing her shattered structure, and the Communists were threatening to gain control through their utopian appeals to humiliated war veterans, much as another dictatorial ideology took control of Germany in 1933. All over the world workers were seeking urgent solutions for their postwar problems. Many were being beguiled by the promises of a new and better life which came to them from the revolution in Russia.

The ILO is truly a "counterrevolutionary" organization. It was created to give an outlet and a hope to working people whose lives, values, and systems had been shattered by the first world war. Offering workers a chance to sit down with employers and governments to find peaceful solutions to their problems, the ILO showed that nations were prepared to deal with labor problems fairly, democratically, and seriously.

The ILO has indeed shown that this can be done.

Thus, from the beginning it has been an important anti-Communist influence. And from the beginning doctrinaire Communists have found the ILO a very uncomfortable place indeed, since they are forced to negotiate about problems which their faith decrees are soluble only by warfare and revolution. Moreover, in the Communist countries there are no employers and free trade unions recognizable by the standards of the rest of the world. Therefore, employer and worker delegates at the ILO have never been wholeheartedly willing to accept Communist representatives. Quite rightly, they consider them no different from government representatives. This basic difference between free and totalitarian countries is a point of continuing strife in the ILO, and while efforts have been made at compromise it is doubtful whether the followers of Marx and Lenin can ever feel at home in the organization.

The issue in conflict is a basic one throughout the world. Freedom of association, freedom to organize unions, and freedom for them to act in the best interests of their members is what many in the newly developing countries have fought and died for. They are prepared to do so again. While there are, as we have seen, varying degrees of state control over trade unions in Asia, Africa, and Latin America, the principles of freedom of association are widely and genuinely accepted, as is the notion of collective bargaining. While it may not be practical in certain countries to adopt our highly developed and independent bargaining patterns, it is, nevertheless, a generally acceptable principle of action.

In the ILO the Communists are forced to disclose the complete lack of freedom for workers which their system demands. They must object at any mention of the right to strike, pointing out that in their "paradise" it is not necessary, but nevertheless leaving a spot of doubt in the minds of the new leaders of the developing world. It has been interesting to see how since 1954, when the Soviet Union reentered the ILO after a long absence, this spot of doubt has spread, and more and more are questioning the sincerity and authenticity of Communist preachments.

Some segments of the American business community, however, notably the National Association of Manufacturers, have been strongly critical of the ILO. They have maintained that the Communists have too much influence in the organization, that it is "socialistic" in its intentions and activities, and that U.S. employers should not be represented at its conferences. In 1961 the NAM refused to send a delegation to the conference and recommended U.S. withdrawal from the organization. Happily the United States Chamber of Commerce took a far more intelligent view and the employers' delegation in 1961 was admirably led by the Chamber's President, Richard Wagner. In his report Mr. Wagner said: "In the battle against totalitarian ideologies, free-world representation—particularly United States employers and workers—did an excellent job of putting the communists on the defensive. As a result, it is my opinion that this year the communists made few or no converts to their unhappy cause." [1]

The accomplishments of the ILO as the first international organization seeking to make social justice the basis of permanent peace were summarized by Pope Pius XII in a special audience for members of the Governing Body in Rome, in 1954:

> Over the past 30 years and more you have patiently and untiringly built up an achievement of which you can justly be proud.
>
> Not only have you contributed to the progress of social legislation in different countries but, above all, you have united governments, employers and workers in courageous and successful collaboration.
>
> You have led them to master every passion, all bitterness in their demands, and every obstinate refusal to face inevitable developments; they have learned to listen to each other's arguments, calmly weigh the facts of an extremely complex problem and jointly propose the necessary improvements.
>
> You have thus created a kind of international forum, a clearing house where essential information and useful ideas are collected, tested and published. [2]

The Work of the ILO

One of the principal activities of the ILO is to formulate international standards covering such things as wages, hours, working conditions, and social legislation. There are

[1] Chamber of Commerce of the United States, *Labor Relations Letter*, Extra Issue, September 1961.
[2] *ILO News*, January 1955.

now more than 230 conventions embodying standards concerning nearly all kinds of labor conditions. The conventions are not binding unless they are accepted by individual national governments; so the ILO is in no sense a world parliament. It is hard to judge how much influence the conventions have had over the years, but in recent times many of the new countries have made use of ILO standards and recommendations in developing employment services, social security plans, safety codes, and other social programs. The United States and many other governments believe that for the present the ILO should not make a major effort to negotiate new conventions. The great need now is for guidance and assistance to nations, particularly those in early stages of development, to give practical effect to the standards already set forth.

Fundamental to all the work of the ILO is the collection and analysis of facts and figures about labor and labor conditions throughout the world. Without doubt the most important single source of such information, the ILO has in recent years given special attention to the collection and improvement of data from the less-developed countries.

The ILO's newest and fastest growing activity is its assistance to nations in Asia, Africa, and Latin America to help their people develop better methods of production, free and peaceful labor relations, more efficient training institutions, and many other necessities for the successful and democratic evolution of an industrially underdeveloped society. Increasingly the ILO is changing its emphasis in order to meet the urgent needs of the more than forty new nations, containing more than one-third of the world's people, which have achieved independent status since World War II. In large numbers they have joined the organization. The primary concern of these nations, David Morse the Director-General points out, "is not with legislation so much as with creating the institutions needed to give a practical content and effect to legislation."[3] These "institutions" are in such fields as vocational training, collective bargaining, employment policy, and social security. Anyone who has seen the ILO at work would be impressed by its ability in these activities, which are of major importance to the solution of the problems raised in earlier chapters of this book.

High in the Andes of Ecuador, Peru, and Bolivia some seven million human beings live short lives at a bare subsistence level, ridden with tuberculosis and other diseases, outside the stream of their nation's life and yet desperately needed to assist in the development of their underpopulated countries. At its field bases in the Andes the ILO in cooperation with other UN agencies, is raising the living standards of these people by teaching them to increase the yield of their crops and training them in carpentry, mechanics, and other skills so that they will be able to contribute to their country's urgent need for skilled manpower. In Haiti, ILO experts taught mechanics how to construct simple windmills, increasing many times the irrigation and power available. They have taught artisans how to make cane knives, introduced the wheelwright's trade, and, by improving tanning methods, revolutionized the leather industry in the whole country.

On the great rivers of Asia, Burma's mighty Irrawaddy, India's holy Ganges, and the age-old Indus of Pakistan, brown-sailed sampans and picturesque paddle wheelers are being steadily replaced by diesel-driven craft. This is largely due to the work of a handful of ILO technicians who have taught mechanics in this Asian region the skills necessary to maintain and repair diesel engines. On an island in the Nile, near Cairo, the ILO has helped to establish a workshop and training center for the blind, the first of its

[3] *The I.L.O. in a Changing World.* Report of the Director-General to the 42nd Session of the International Labor Conference (Geneva: ILO, 1958), p. 2.

kind in the country. In Ceylon, Brazil, Guatemala, and Indonesia assistance is being given for the rehabilitation of the physically handicapped.

Following the disastrous methane gas explosions in the coal mines of Zonguldak, Turkey, Turkish miners and safety engineers visited France, Great Britain, and Germany under ILO worker training programs to find out how to prevent such disasters from recurring. India's capital city, New Delhi, plagued by breakdowns in the public transportation system, called upon the ILO for help. A productivity expert showed the Indians how to expedite repair and maintenance procedures, which solved the problem. ILO productivity teams have helped repeatedly to increase productivity in India, Pakistan, and a score of other countries around the world.

These are just a few examples of hundreds of ILO technical assistance projects being carried out around the world under both the United Nations Expanded Program of Technical Assistance and the ILO's own regular programs. The ILO does not undertake elaborate projects costing a lot of money. Often it simply provides single experts who work under extremely difficult conditions to teach new skills in isolated communities. The ILO's funds are very limited and it uses them carefully where they will have the greatest impact in supporting, not substituting for, going programs. As quickly as it can, the ILO tries to get out of any given project and leave it to the people themselves to carry it on.

Obviously the importance of such work to the development of free, vigorous economies is beyond measure. It is hard to conceive of any more effective way in which to discourage, in a thoroughly constructive fashion, the subversion of democracy by dictatorship.

More can be done, however. The United States should encourage the ILO to step up its activities in agriculture.

Traditionally, the ILO has concentrated most heavily on the problems of urban and industrial workers. Only recently has it extended its work to rural areas. Peasants and landless masses are prime targets for Marxist-Leninist subversion and control. Their needs are extreme and they are beginning to try to break out of the miserable conditions in which they have lived for so many years. They are ripe for revolution. The ILO can help make that revolution a useful and productive one which will lead to reform, freedom, and a better way of life rather than violence, bloodshed, and another form of serfdom.

Specifically, the ILO should be encouraged to increase the help it gives to the formation of cooperatives, especially in rural areas, and, where possible, as part of worker organizations. Unfortunately in many developing countries there has been futile feuding between ILO technical assistance operations and U.S. aid activities. Over the years a considerable amount of friction between the ILO and the predecessors of AID has developed, mostly of a jurisdictional and bureaucratic nature, which, of course, accomplishes nothing. It would appear that in the development of cooperatives, in which until recently U.S. aid agencies had almost no interest and little experience, the United States might well encourage the ILO to become the major operator around the world. The ILO has had remarkable success in assisting the formation of cooperatives in several parts of the developing world, especially Southeast Asia. It can draw technicians from Scandinavian and other European countries which have had far wider and more varied experience of cooperatives than the United States has had. And it can reach into areas where for political reasons our aid and technicians may not be always welcome.

Another important field of work in which the United States might encourage increased ILO activity is the development of what have come to be called high-level human resources, or leadership groups in newly developing countries—managers, foremen, supervisors, and the like. There are many instances in which important operations have failed or been seriously delayed because of a lack of a handful of managers. The steel mill at Rourkela, India, for example, was built and finished, but lay idle many months for lack of about twenty top executives. The Indian government asked the United States for help and oddly enough we were unable to supply the necessary men. This problem is widespread and requires early planning at all stages of manpower development. The ILO, drawing on the skills and talents of the entire world, could be of real assistance here.

One of the most important aspects of the ILO's work is its effect on the growth of free labor institutions and practices in the developing countries of Asia, Africa, and Latin America. Through its field offices and countless contacts with trade unionists throughout the world, the ILO can have a very important influence on workers' organizations. Workers' education programs teach the basic elements of collective bargaining, the responsibilities of a trade union, and the methods of negotiation, and provide the basis for the development of peaceful understanding between employer and employee. There is education, too, in the annual conference of the ILO, a unique meeting place for the leaders of labor from all over the world. It is the only opportunity many have to travel from their country and be exposed to government, employer, and worker representatives of other countries. The conference thus provides an extremely important opportunity for the exchange of views and the promotion of understanding between various sections of the world.

One of the things these workers' leaders can see firsthand at the conference is the hypocrisy of the Communist claims and preachments. For example, in 1956 and 1957 the annual conference considered the problem of forced labor and adopted a standard in the form of a convention condemning the practice and calling for its elimination. The Soviet Union quite naturally was peculiarly sensitive on this subject, since several years earlier the United Nations and the ILO had found that forced labor existed on a very wide scale in the U.S.S.R. and other Communist-bloc countries. This was something which was not particularly harmonious with the Communist claims to a workers' paradise. Since workers are supposed to be the most fortunate people in Marxian utopia, it was particularly useful that in the ILO debate the falsity of the Communist claims was most effectively exposed by labor delegates, and not by governmental representatives alone.

For example, at the same time that he denied the existence of forced labor in the U.S.S.R. the Soviet delegate referred to the Taft-Hartley Act as a "slave labor act." The American worker delegate, Mr. George P. Delaney, rose from his seat flushed with anger and, in a way a governmental spokesman could hardly have managed, castigated the Russian. He said American labor objected to certain portions of the Taft-Hartley Act and hoped to get it changed, but he forcefully denied that it had anything to do with "slave labor." He then proceeded to list in great detail the embarrassing evidence of real slave labor which then existed behind the Iron Curtain. This struck far deeper in the minds of many at the conference than a governmental response.

At a more recent session of the ILO conference, Rudolph Faupl, the American worker delegate, urged with authority the rejection of the credentials of the Hungarian delegation. Faupl, who was born in Hungary, came to the United States as a young boy; a machinist by trade, he is widely respected by his fellow workers around the world. With stirring emotion he spoke of the ruthless suppression of the workers of Hungary. For two years in succession the entire Hungarian delegation was refused admission.

At the annual meeting in Geneva in June of 1959 I had the honor to sponsor a resolution with the Minister of Labor of India, Gulzarilal Nanda, calling upon the ILO to increase its operational and technical assistance activities in a number of fields. The resolution was adopted unanimously with the exception of the Soviet bloc. Their objections to it were difficult to understand, but undoubtedly they found it impossible to endorse the expansion of ILO's activities in the promotion of free, democratic institutions of labor relations. It was perplexing for many of those from the newer countries, who have taken seriously the Communist line, to learn that they were opposed to expanding programs which are of such vital and immediate importance to the newly developing countries.

During 1961, the ILO's new Institute for Labor Studies opened its doors for leaders from all over the world who are concerned with labor problems. The Institute will provide a forum where workers' leaders from Asia, Africa, and Latin America can come and seek from each other the answers to some of the difficult questions confronting them and their organizations, such as: What in fact is the role of a trade union in a country where necessity demands a high degree of national savings and where the needs of economic growth may preclude immediate wage increases? How can a union aid its membership and maintain its strength and effectiveness by engaging in the economic development process? What needs to be done to enable a union to contribute to the total wealth of the country as well as to the needs of its members, by itself building houses, making clothes, or distributing food?

Managers may come to the new Institute and ask: How can we provide the production and industrial initiative so vital to economic growth and at the same time ensure social justice in our plants, factories, and fields? What are the mechanics of labor relations most suited to our problems and requirements? How can we best strengthen that system of freedom and democracy upon which successful enterprise depends? At the same time, government officials and political leaders may be examining questions of great concern to them. What is the optimum relationship between government, management, and labor? When does the heavy hand of bureaucracy stifle and extinguish the priceless vigor arising from free processes, and when does it encourage, stabilize, and protect that vigor and those processes? In what circumstances do labor and social problems require governmental intervention and the use of special powers?

If this Institute is successful, it can add a new dimension to the ILO's service to less-developed countries. It is financed largely from an endowment fund to which many countries, developed and less-developed, have made generous contributions. As yet, the United States has given nothing.

The Institute is the newest in the series of activities by which the ILO is contributing substantially to the improvement of labor conditions and practices in less-developed countries. As I have argued throughout this book, the United States should be intensifying its efforts to help in the growth of free trade unions throughout the world. It follows that we should be giving as much support as we possibly can to the ILO, for it works toward the same end.

There is still another way in which the ILO's work in raising labor standards abroad helps the United States. David Morse alluded to it in this fashion:

> An implicit purpose of the early ILO was to prevent any country and particularly the less industrialized countries, from entering into international trade competition on the basis of cheap labor standards. . . . Our main emphasis today is on improving working and living conditions by helping the less

advanced countries to develop their economic potential and to raise their productivity and by helping the more advanced countries to lay the social basis for greater economic cooperation.

As living standards rise in the rest of the world, purchasing power will increase and with it the potential market for American exports. The rise of labor standards abroad tends to reduce the disparity between foreign and American labor costs, thereby improving the competitive position of American goods on world markets. Unless this kind of progress is made it may become increasingly difficult to continue improving the incomes of American workers. These are long-run considerations, but they should not be left out of account at a time when changes in our trade and balance of payments have taught us that the United States must be highly conscious of its costs of production in a competitive world.

The ILO and United States Policy

The ILO after forty-three years stands today at the threshold of vast opportunity and represents a bright hope to many millions of people throughout the world. It has come a long way since that day in 1919 when representatives from forty nations met in Washington at the first conference. It has shown itself adjustable to change and sensitive to the new needs which confront it. It is an organization of people, a human organization working through and among people for the attainment of certain human goals. "It is," to quote Mr. Morse again, "neither the embodiment of an absolute moral law revealed forty years ago and enshrined in the Constitution, nor is it a supra-national judicial authority empowered to enforce certain defined standards. The ILO works in the world as it finds it and it works in the world for the attainment of its purpose. This purpose . . . is the improvement of conditions of men and women throughout the world."

Strong participation in the ILO gives the United States a unique opportunity to prove its devotion to the high ideals of social justice upon which the organization was founded. It gives us an opportunity to heed seriously and act on the admonition contained in the ILO constitution that "conditions of labour exist involving such injustice, hardship and privation to large numbers of people as to produce unrest so great that the peace and harmony of the world are imperilled. . . ." I have pointed out some of the specific reasons the ILO is important to the United States in our effort to strengthen free labor all over the world. There is very good cause to believe that it will be even more important in the years ahead.

The outcome of the enormous struggle of hundreds of millions of people in the newly developing areas of the world for economic improvement and freedom from foreign domination will undoubtedly determine the course of the world in years to come. There has probably never been such a huge and important mass emotion as the determined desire of the people of the developing nations for an improvement in their way of life. The International Labor Organization is looked to as a principal contributor to the fulfillment of these needs. If these desires are not going to be frustrated and if the world is going to avoid the terrible consequences of such frustration—the bitter resentment of the poor toward the rich, of the have-nots toward the haves, of the downtrodden toward the exalted—then we must strengthen the ILO in every possible way. If we do, it will continue its admirable efforts to meet today's problems, human dignity will be enhanced, the cause of freedom will prosper, and the world will be a little closer to peace.

Chapter IX

THE PROTECTION
OF REVOLUTION

The general proposition of this book is that organizations of workers are a powerful force, seriously affecting the fulfillment of our foreign policy in the developing world. Further, it is that American labor, management, and government must urgently improve their approach to this force.

Though I have concentrated on proposals for making our policies more effective, I have also alluded to some of the difficulties we are bound to encounter. Some of them stem from the fact that at any given moment U.S. policy is likely to have a number of different immediate purposes in each part of the world. For instance, we sometimes have to work rather closely with dictatorial regimes, for military or other reasons. How far can we go to build up free trade unions if that course is anathema to the dictator? Other difficulties stem from the limits of our power abroad. Even if we are not going out of our way to gain favor with a particular government, how great is our ability to aid the growth of democratic unions where they are suppressed?

There can be no universally valid answer to such questions; their equivalents arise in almost every part of foreign policy. Sometimes part of the answer to them will lie in a consideration of what can be done by American business and labor, which do not work under the same constraints as government. There are circumstances in which American unions can be far more effective in encouraging a strong, non-Communist worker movement than our government. Likewise the policies of many American companies abroad can sometimes have a more important and far-reaching effect on worker organizations than can governmental action. But, of course, American labor and business abroad are also limited in what they can do. Foreign laws, regulations, and political pressure restrict their activities. Companies, however enlightened they may be, have to give their main attention to the conduct of their business. The resources of the labor movement for foreign programs are limited.

We must also face the fact that the pluralistic character of our society—which can enhance our performance abroad in some of the ways I have indicated—has the corollary that business and labor will not always agree with the government's policy. They may use what influence they have in a direction contrary to that which Washington prefers; in any case, they cannot be expected to lend themselves to a course of action they disapprove. In matters as complicated as those of foreign labor, in which even the desirability or undesirability of a certain development is open to honest differences of judgment, such conflicts of interest or opinion are bound to be frequent. We would not have it otherwise. There are advantages, too, in showing the world that our society and polity are truly free, democratic, and pluralistic. Yet there is nothing to be gained by ignoring the complications introduced into our policy by our very nature.

All this is by way of caution and the recognition of the complications inherent in our function in the world. None of these difficulties detract from the need to increase our efforts to pursue a clear, farsighted, and effective international labor policy.

The Question of "Intervention"

How can the United States effectively concern itself with the development of free trade unions in foreign countries without becoming hopelessly involved in the distasteful process of intervening in the domestic affairs of another country? The question is usually asked by traditionalists who are captivated by the idea of "aid without strings," and who believe that the United States should avoid at all costs tampering with the internal affairs of other countries. The fact is, of course, that much as we might like to, it is practically impossible for the United States today to have any important kind of relations with another country, especially in the form of a highly developed aid program, without having a profound influence on that country's internal affairs. In this sense it is impossible not to "intervene" though we may abjure the kind of action that has been stigmatized by the older, more traditional use of that term: introducing military force into another country or, at a minimum, using whatever power we could muster directly to impose one political regime or to prevent another from assuming office.

All U.S. operations in the developing world—the American company, our labor movement, or our governmental programs—have some sort of influence for good or bad on the countries where they take place. Otherwise they are ineffective. Too often in the past we have adopted the head-in-the-sand attitude of saying to ourselves: we as a government are dealing simply with the government of the recipient country; we are giving it only the aid it requests; we are waiting passively for such requests; our companies in this country are an extension of American private enterprise, and are beyond the scope of U.S. government influence;

therefore, their activities cannot be expected to take account of the national interest in any decisive way; similarly, our labor unions are private, voluntary organizations which have a right to engage in their private, voluntary activities around the world.

Even if this reasoning were valid so far as our own ideas about ourselves are concerned, it would be misleading because others do not see us in the same way. The people of Africa, Asia, and Latin America regard every activity, governmental and nongovernmental, which has its roots in the United States, as American. No matter what distinctions are made, we must recognize that every American activity has an influence in one direction or another. If a corrupt, dictatorial, or antilabor government receives aid funds from us, and if these funds are spent without the most careful policy guidance from the United States, they may well do more harm than good. Even though the projects on which the funds are spent may appear to be technically sound, involving the construction of needed dams, housing projects, or irrigation systems, the expenditures may be regarded by the people, and more particularly the worker organizations, as helping a basically unpopular regime and blocking the long-term advancement of more democratic forces. Consequently, we have to realize that every action by an American abroad affects the national interest. Our influence and power are great. Try as we may to divorce ourselves from them or slip some of the responsibility off onto a host government, as a practical matter we cannot get away with it.

Let us not pretend that we are a small, antiseptic power which can go from country to country distributing hundreds of millions of dollars without having an influence on the internal affairs of those countries. Let us rather extend and broaden the reasoning behind the Act of Bogotá and the Alliance for Progress. In these programs, for the first time, we formally tied to our aid the string of social justice. We made our material contribution dependent on a spiritual or ideological commitment as well as a practical one. We exercised leadership. President Eisenhower and President Kennedy after him proclaimed our alliance with reform.

In this same way we should use our vast influence, as appropriate, to encourage the regimes of newly developing countries to foster those actions and programs which will encourage the growth of strong, non-Communist worker organizations. We should point out to these regimes that such encouragement is necessary for their own protection from subversion, disruption, and overthrow. Let us not be bashful about setting forth our purposes. Many of our problems around the world today arise from our strange reluctance to proclaim forcefully what we think is right.

This is perhaps natural because our international history is checkered with instances in which various of our spokesmen have proclaimed what is wrong, usually out of ignorance or misunderstanding. For a long period, for example, we seemed to be encouraging newly developing countries to adopt our economic system intact without ourselves even understanding in full what that system is, much less the difficulties inherent in its transplantation to other countries. For a time we had only a superficial understanding of the neutralism of such countries as India. There are still those who proclaim—too loudly in my view—that military assistance is the key to the defense of freedom and that economic and social assistance is money down the drain. Experience in places like Laos tends to prove that the opposite is true. This kind of blundering has given us an understandable lack of self-confidence. But such failures to understand international problems are not surprising, since we as a nation have really only been thinking about them in any sustained way since World War II. Hopefully we are now informed and sophisticated enough to be able with confidence to say where we

234/ The Protection of Revolution

stand in the world's revolutionary struggle in which we are deeply involved.

Our Place in a Revolutionary Process

Another question which can be legitimately asked about the basic argument of this book is whether there is not a good chance that once a strong worker organization has been built in a particular country, the Communists might not come along and take it over. Are we, in short, building Frankenstein monsters by encouraging the development of trade unions in the developing world?

This is a real danger. But the alternative of discouraging, or through nonaction appearing to discourage, the growth of unions is far more dangerous. Worker organizations will inevitably develop in the countries of Asia, Africa, and Latin America. Their creation and growth arises out of deeply felt political and economic need; their continued importance is sure. If we do not help them, less desirable powers will. Furthermore, as we have seen in our own society as well as others, strong, responsible worker organizations are a necessity for the development of a successful democratic society. They are by nature and purpose opposed to tyranny and oppression; they are a leading force in the revolutionary process now going forward in the developing world. As such they are our natural allies provided we and they see our real long-run interests clearly.

Our central task in the underdeveloped areas, as W. W. Rostow has said, is to protect the independence in which the revolutionary process can take place.

> This is our mission, and it is our ultimate strength. For this is not—and cannot be—the mission of communism. . . . Despite all the Communist talk of aiding movements of national independence, they are driven in the end, by the nature of their system, to violate the independence of nations. Despite

all the Communist talk of American imperialism, we are committed, by the nature of our system, to support the cause of national independence. And the truth will out.[1]

It will, I think, provided we do more than we have up to now to establish ourselves as leaders in the revolution at work in the southern half of the world today. It will if we heed the call of Henry M. Wriston and others to realize the central role we can play in this Age of Revolution, which started in 1776 and is by no means over in 1962. As Mr. Wriston says, "the first necessity is to rid ourselves of nervousness when 'revolution' is mentioned. Politicians often shy like horses at the mere word." [2]

We should remember the words of Thomas Jefferson: "What country before ever existed a century and a half without a revolution? . . . the tree of liberty must be refreshed from time to time with the blood of patriots and tyrants. It is its natural manure." We should recall that part of our Declaration of Independence which says: "That whenever any Form of Government becomes destructive of these ends, it is the Right of the People to alter or to abolish it, and to institute a new Government, laying its foundation on such principles and organizing its powers in such form, as to them shall seem most likely to effect their Safety and Happiness."

After all, we were the ones who made the word "revolution" honorable. The great movement for a rising standard of living, for freedom, and for dignity, which is sweeping throughout the southern half of the world is really a global echo of that great proclamation which says that all men are created equal and have certain rights to life, liberty, and the pursuit of happiness. Let us boldly assert our relation to it

[1] W. W. Rostow, address at graduation ceremonies at the U.S. Army Special Warfare School, June 28, 1961; reprinted in *The Department of State Bulletin*, August 7, 1961, p. 235.

[2] Henry M. Wriston, "The Age of Revolution," *Foreign Affairs*, July 1961, p. 535.

and seek in all ways to protect its just causes; to extend it and to make the Declaration of Independence the international doctrine our founding fathers meant it to be.

Around the newly developing world this is the business of many worker organizations. It is partly in the light of our heritage that they are moving. Let us not abdicate or renounce what may be our most significant contribution to civilization: the sacred right of revolution. Let us not obscure our purposes by any queasy lingering on bureaucratic form, persisting in the illusion that we can avoid any responsibility for what goes on in those countries which we are heavily supporting. Let us not balk at the word "intervention." What if France in 1776 had shirked from intervention? We might well have lost *our* revolution. Let us rather back up with prudent action our high declarations of loyalty to the cause of freedom, democracy, and social justice wherever and whenever it may be in jeopardy.

We face an adversary in the world today with few scruples about intervention; with little concern for the forms of the past; with an unerring confidence that his way is the way of history and that all save it will topple. With zeal and dedication the Communist pursues his course, more reactionary than revolutionary, more oppressive than liberal. We must not let him steal the title of leader in the revolution for freedom and reform. It belongs to us; let us make the most of it.

We must never let the crisis of the moment or the threat of military conflict so preoccupy us that we lose sight of the fact that communism does not intend to conquer the world primarily through military means. While it resorts to violence here and there to create unrest and promote disruption, it relies on the operation of economic and social forces within the non-Communist world to spread its control. It seeks to use the revolution for its imperialistic ends. In this respect it is a most untraditional enemy and requires an entirely new response from those who would defeat it. That response, as we have seen, must include the construction of a framework of economic and social strength to protect the independence of the revolutionary process going on around the world. Worker organizations are a crucial part of this framework and should have a central place in the foreign relations of American labor, management, and government.

INDEX

Accra Conference (1952); *see* All-African Trade Union Federation

Act of Bogotá, 232-33

Adams, John Clarke, *6n*

Adams, Samuel, 18

Adoula, Cyrille, 37

Africa, 31-38

anti-Communist influences on labor, 76, 77, 84, 110, 117; *see also* African Regional Organization

authoritarianism in governments, 37-38

government control of unions, 38, 116-17

governments as employers of wage labor, 34, 76-77

labor support for independence, 32-35, 47

labor union federations; *see* UGTAN, AATUF, ICATU, ATUC

political influence of labor, 34-37

problems of trade unions, 31, 37-38

African Regional Organization (AFRO), 71-72

African Trade Union Confederation (ATUC), 62

Afro-Asian Institute for Labor Studies and Cooperation, 49, 84, 187

Agency for International Development (AID), *6n*, 113, 171-73, 179, 180-81, 222

Ahmedabad Textile Labor Association, 39-40, 104, 119, 121, 123

Algeria

anti-Communist influences on labor, 71, 84

political importance of labor, 35

All-Africa People's Conference, 34

All-African Trade Union Federation (AATUF), 33, 61, 101

Accra Conference (1959), 61

Casablanca Conference (1961), 61-62

All-China Federation of Trade Unions (ACFTU), 64

Alliance for Progress, 232-33

All-India Trade Union Congress (AITUC), 20, 40-41, 64

All-Indonesian Central Labor Organization (SOBSI), 42-45, 64

238